Y0-DBZ-985

Salt from the Psalter

GOLDEN GATE SEMINARY LIBRARY

SALT from the PSALTER

Mary Frances Owens

BROADMAN PRESS Nashville, Tennessee

GOLDEN GATE SEMINARY LIBRARY

BS
1430.3
O9
c.4

©Copyright 1980 • Broadman Press.

All rights reserved.

4212-18

ISBN: 0-8054-1218-2

Verses marked RSV are from the Revised Standard Version of the Bible, copyrighted 1946, 1952, © 1971, 1973.

Verses marked TEV are from the *Good News Bible,* the Bible in Today's English Version. Old Testament: Copyright © American Bible Society, 1976; New Testament: Copyright © American Bible Society, 1966; 1971, 1976. Used by permission.

Verses marked NEB are from *The New English Bible.* Copyright © The Delegates of the Oxford University Press and the Syndics of the Cambridge University Press, 1961, 1970. Reprinted by permission.

Dewey Decimal Classification: 232.2

Subject heading: BIBLE O. T. PSALMS

Library of Congress Catalog Card Number: 80-67147

Printed in the United States of America

To my children
Kay, Sue, and Tim
who have seasoned my life with joy.

CONTENTS

Introduction 9

Chapter 1
The Righteous Man **Assesses Happiness** 13

Chapter 2
The Righteous Man **Faces Affliction** 26

Chapter 3
The Righteous Man **Exults in Faith** 40

Chapter 4
The Righteous Man **Copes with Doubt** 54

Chapter 5
The Righteous Man **Interprets Nature** 67

Chapter 6
The Righteous Man **Responds to Success** 79

Chapter 7
The Righteous Man **Contends with Failure** 91

Chapter 8
The Righteous Man **Participates in Government** 105

Chapter 9
The Righteous Man **Communes with God** 117

Summary 133

Introduction

Salt has a long and fascinating history, not only as a substance but also as a figure of speech. Since man's early beginnings on earth, salt has been essential for survival. Scientists say that without at least a trace of salt in some form, man could not survive much longer than a month. Salt is contained in our blood plasma. Without it, our body cells would die.

Most students of history and science recognize the secular value of salt in ancient days. It exerted a considerable economic influence on society long before the advent of Christ. Because of its great importance as a preservative and seasoning, it literally served as money. The term *salary* stems from the word *salt.* A wealthy man possessed a lot of salt.

Ancient people thought that salt had special sacred power. Orientals used it to ward off evil, protect the dead, and bring good fortune to newlyweds. These uses of salt probably stemmed from the belief that something that important must have power beyond face value.

Of more interest to Jews and Christians, however, is the fact that from early times Hebrew culture was steeped in the symbolism of salt. Some of the symbolic references to salt in the Old Testament sound very strange. For example, to "eat a man's salt" meant to be a guest in the household. The sharing of a meal automatically implied that the host would protect his guest. Ezekiel 16:4 speaks of the rubbing of newborn babies with salt. Another passage, 2 Kings 2:19-22, tells of Elisha's throwing salt into a bad spring of water to make it sweet.

One of the most significant, yet little explored, uses of the symbolism of salt in the Old Testament is that of the "covenant of salt." This "covenant of salt" referred to the binding of two parties (God and Israel) in an irrevocable pact. The Israelites acknowledged that their covenant was inviolable by literally salting their sacrifices. Leviticus 2:13; Numbers 18:19; and 2 Chronicles 13:5 make direct references to this practice. Ezra 6:9 includes salt in the list of provisions for the Temple. Ezekiel 43:24 refers to the sprinkling of salt on rams and bulls to be sacrificed as burnt offering. Exodus 30:35 (Revised Standard Version) tells of incense being seasoned with salt.

The fact that the Old Testament used salt symbolically suggests that Jesus' disciples had likely heard of the imagery of salt long before Jesus said, "Ye are the salt of the earth" (Matt. 5:13). The figure of salt had its origin in the Old Testament, but Jesus applied fresh meaning to it.

When Jesus spoke of the disciples as salt, he referred to their function in the world. They must counteract the insipidness of an apathetic society. They must become a positive, zestful seasoning. They must be a preservative element in a decaying world. In short, they must be like salt, exerting a power disproportionate to their quantity. Just as a little salt can go a long way, so must a few disciples make a powerful impact on a large segment of humanity.

The major theme of this book is that the psalmist became an Old Testament forerunner of the disciples whom Christ called *salt*. He represented the true worshiper of his day and will be referred to in this book primarily as "the righteous man of the Psalter." This righteous man acted as salt in his own day. His pervading influence for good in the ancient world served in a seasoning and preservative capacity. The man described in the Psalter had not yet been refined to the degree of the "salt" of the Christian era. Nevertheless, he functioned according to the best knowledge of the era in which he lived.

It would be less than honest to ignore the presence of some psalms in the Psalter that run contrary to Christian ideals. The so-called imprecatory psalms (prayers for vengeance upon enemies and rejoicing at their destruction) conflict with the later teachings of Christ. We must keep in mind, however, that the psalmist did not have the benefit of the gospel and the enlightenment provided by Christ's interpretation of righteousness. He tried to live according to the best light of his time. In spite of his human weaknesses, the righteous man of the Psalter emerged as a basically God-fearing, devoted worshiper whose saltness became manifest to all who observed him.

The people of Jesus' day treasured the Psalter; in fact, Jesus himself quoted from the Psalter on several occasions. It remains a much revered book of the Bible today. Its inspiring and deeply spiritual nature makes it a popular and useful book of meditations. The Psalter reflects the personal and corporate worship experiences of God's people, sometimes arrived at only after great anguish, but climaxed with expressions of joy and inner peace. Its exuberant praise of, and confident trust in the Lord make it a worthy model of devotion for our own times.

The psalms selected for discussion in this book reveal a preservative and zestful element in ancient society. We shall look briefly at some of the experiences of life which reveal the saltness of the righteous man of the Psalms. We shall see how he assessed happiness, faced affliction, exulted in faith, coped with doubt, interpreted nature, responded to success, contended with failure, participated in government, and communed with God. At the end of each of the studies you will find a brief application of the Psalm to modern life. I hope that these twenty-seven studies will inspire you to delve more deeply into the spiritual relevance and meaning of the Psalms.

Except where otherwise indicated, the King James Version of the Bible has been used in this study. Its beauty of expression, especially in dealing with the Psalms, has earned it a place of special favor in the hearts of many Christians. In a few instances, however, quotations from the Revised Standard Version have been used. This was done in order to clarify the meaning of certain expressions in the commentary material which have changed in usage since the earlier version was translated.

Two of the books that especially helped me gain insights into the meaning of the Psalter are *The Psalms* by Artur Weiser (translated by Herbert Hartwell and published by Westminster Press) and *The Psalms* by A. F. Kirkpatrick (from the Cambridge Bible for Schools and Colleges, published by the University Press at Cambridge). A special acknowledgment goes to my husband, J. J. Owens, who is professor of Old Testament Interpretation at Southern Baptist Theological Seminary. His ability to make the Old Testament, particularly the Psalms, come alive, inspired me to want to write this book.

Jesus Christ must remain our final authority in the interpretation of what it means to be salt in the Christian era. Nevertheless, we can learn much from the psalmist of long ago about the saltness of righteous persons of any generation. One of the lessons is that piety can be a thing of joy. With the psalmist, "Let us come before his presence with thanksgiving, and make a joyful noise unto him with psalms . . . for the Lord is a great God" (Ps. 95:2-3).

Chapter 1
The Righteous Man
Assesses Happiness

Psalm 1

[1]Blessed is the man that walketh not in the counsel of the ungodly, nor standeth in the way of sinners, nor sitteth in the seat of the scornful.

[2]But his delight is in the law of the Lord; and in his law doth he meditate day and night.

[3]And he shall be like a tree planted by the rivers of water, that bringeth forth his fruit in his season; his leaf also shall not wither; and whatsoever he doeth shall prosper.

[4]The ungodly are not so: but are like the chaff which the wind driveth away.

[5]Therefore the ungodly shall not stand in the judgment, nor sinners in the congregation of the righteous.

[6]For the Lord knoweth the way of the righteous: but the way of the ungodly shall perish.

As we browse through the many beautiful and inspiring psalms contained in the Psalter, we may wonder how the compiler happened to select Psalm 1 as a prologue to the book. Several other psalms far surpass it in poetic beauty. Why did the compilers not use another psalm instead? The answer to these questions has importance to our understanding of the whole book.

Psalm 1 serves as an ideal prologue for the book because it briefly sums up the teachings and beliefs of the entire Psalter. It assumes from the beginning that Yahweh (God) is in control of the world, and that because he is holy and just, he rewards those who keep his commandments. This theme is basic to all other themes in the book.

Nevertheless, quite clearly the righteous man described in Psalm 1 becomes the conscience through which God's people collectively view and assess the experiences of life. (As explained in the introduction, the expression *righteous man* will be used throughout the book to denote a representative of the true worshiper in the psalmist's time.) In Psalms 1, 128, and 84, the righteous man demonstrated one aspect of his saltness: the happiness which permeates his life and has a preservative influence in the community. We will take a brief look at those three psalms in this chapter.

Psalm 1 focuses on one special source of the righteous man's happiness: he has learned the superiority of God's law over the example and advice of unrighteous people. The word *blessed* (v. 1) literally means "O how happy!" Happy is the person who knows the difference between temporal and lasting pleasure, and pursues the way of godliness.

In this decade many people have explored the topic of what happiness is. If we believed the barrage of cartoons on the subject, we would expect to find lasting happiness in everything from having our backs rubbed to having our children wash their hands without being asked. The psalmist took a much more serious view of happiness than this. He viewed happiness as a life and death matter: the good life for the righteous man; punishment and death for the evil man.

The righteous man of the Psalter conceived of happiness as both an outer and inner experience. Outwardly, the righteous man would receive as a reward for his goodness a prosperity in all his activities. Inwardly, he would enjoy the security of a close relationship with God. However, these rewards would not come without deliberate effort.

Notice in verse 1 the negative restrictions that the righteous man must observe for true happiness. He must not take the counsel of *ungodly* persons, for acceptance of their advice can lead only to disharmony with God, self, and other persons. He must not adopt the way of life of persistent *sinners* (those who habitually miss the mark spiritually). They have already proved their moral failure through their constant sinning. He must not have any dealings with the *scornful* (those who mock God and right living). One could not find worse people in the world to look to as guides for life than those mentioned above.

Now observe the positive stance the righteous man takes in verse 2. He not only obeys and meditates on the teachings of God—he finds delight in doing so. He recognizes that God knows better than man the path which will lead to true happiness. Therefore, instead of resenting the law, he treasures it. It becomes to him a shield and protector rather than a threat to his freedom. He shares the conviction of one who said, "Happy are you, O Israel! Who is like you,/a people saved by the Lord,/the shield of your help,/and the sword of your triumph!" (Deut. 33:29, RSV).

Verse 3 pictures the righteous man as a tree, planted by rivers of water. Like a tree that depends on water for sustenance, so the righteous man depends on the stream of God's grace for nourishment and refreshment. He bears the fruit of uprightness; his vitality does not die. He prospers (lit., carries through to a successful conclusion) whatever he attempts.

In contrast to the righteous man, the ungodly man has no roots and nothing to sustain him. Instead of standing like a strong tree, this evil man becomes like the chaff which the wind blows away (v. 4). Because of his worthless quality, the ungodly will not hold his ground when God separates the righteous from the wicked. Likewise, the habitual sinner will find himself separated from the congregation of the righteous when God purges and purifies it (v. 5).

The writer draws the conclusion that God is a just God. The words "the Lord knoweth" (v. 6) have the connotation of caring. The Lord not only approves of and guides the righteous man, he also cares about him in tender, loving concern. The ungodly man, however, faces a different outcome. Instead of letting God's laws guide his life, he has deliberately cut out his own path—a path that can only lead to destruction. "The Lord watches over the way of the righteous,/but the way of the wicked is doomed" (v. 6, NEB).

Here, then, we see the example of a righteous man who found his happiness in knowing and doing the revealed will of God. He recognized the keeping of God's law as a religious duty, but he loved it so much that it became a source of happiness to him. Like salt, the good man maintained a preservative function in the world by setting an example of true happiness for others to follow.

People of today often find that happiness is an elusive quality to capture. One of the reasons is that they pursue it in the wrong places. People look for happiness in money and possessions, but they soon discover that wealth alone carries no guarantee of lasting satisfaction. They seek for happiness in adulterous relationships, but find the "forbidden fruit" less pleasant than they anticipated. They endeavor to capture happiness by improving their health through strict diet and exercise programs, hoping to lengthen their life span. Often, however, they discover that quantity of life does not necessarily imply quality, or that physical health alone will not fill all their needs. In their search for happiness, people may even succeed in progressing from nothingness to fame, only to find life lonely and precarious at the top.

Where, then, can persons of our day find the enduring, salty zest in life for which they long? The psalmist gave some straightforward advice on the subject that still applies today. Look to the right sources for advice; follow the example of godly people; become so rooted in righteousness that your spiritual life can flourish (vv. 1-3). By correctly assessing the difference between temporary and lasting pleasure and pursuing those goals that have permanent value, persons will find a satisfying existence. Happy is the person who looks to the Lord for guidance, for he will receive spiritual prosperity.

Psalm 128

¹**Blessed is every one that feareth the Lord; that walketh in his ways.**

²**For thou shalt eat the labour of thine hands: happy shalt thou be, and it shall be well with thee.**

³**Thy wife shall be as a fruitful vine by the sides of thine house: thy children like olive plants round about thy table.**

⁴**Behold, that thus shall the man be blessed that feareth the Lord.**

⁵**The Lord shall bless thee out of Zion: and thou shalt see the good of Jerusalem all the days of thy life.**

⁶**Yea, thou shalt see thy children's children, and peace upon Israel.**

In the study of Psalm 1 we noted that one reason for the righteous man's happiness was that he recognized the superiority of God's law over the example and advice of unrighteous people. He listened to God (a proven success) instead of sinful persons (proven failures).

Psalm 128 changes the focus slightly from the reason for the worshiper's happiness to the way that his happiness manifested itself. In assessing happiness, the psalmist takes into consideration the fact that one aspect of happiness is the ability to enjoy things that we often take for granted. He focuses, in this psalm, on three blessings: work, family, and hope for the nation.

Work, the first of the three blessings, brings to mind several thoughts. Although not brought out directly in the psalm, the opportunity and ability to work are great blessings in themselves. Until faced with unemployment or disability, a person does not usually fully appreciate the privilege of work. However, Psalm 128 does bring out another thought concerning the blessings of work: that of being able to enjoy the fruits of one's labor.

The second blessing, family, held a place of high priority as a source of happiness. Martin Luther called Psalm 128 a "Marriage Song" because of its emphasis on the joy of family life. Certainly part of a righteous man's saltness was his example in the home—his love for family, his gratitude to God for them, and his spiritual leadership of them. But he also considered his wife and children a reward for his righteousness. Conversely, he interpreted lack of children in the home as a sign of God's disapproval and disfavor.

The third blessing, hope for the nation, was very precious to every Israelite. The happiness of the individual had a close relationship to the prosperity (both material and spiritual) of the nation as a whole. Today, Christians might say: As go the homes, so goes the nation. The ancient Israelite would be more likely to say: As goes the nation, so go the homes. The hope of the individual and his family rested in God's blessing on the nation. The true worshiper cared very much what happened to the nation as a whole. Like salt, the worshiper served in a preservative capacity in a nation that frequently failed to follow God's teachings.

The title of Psalm 128, "A Song of Degrees" (KJV) or "A Song of Ascents" (RSV) suggests its later usage by Israel. Some scholars believe Psalm 128 to be one of a collection of psalms sung by the Israelite worshipers as they traveled to Jerusalem for feast days. From other Scriptures, such as Isaiah 30:29 and Psalm 42:4, we know that the pilgrims sang on their pilgrimage to Jerusalem.

Verse 1 begins with a truth that becomes the foundation for all else that the psalmist intends to say: "Blessed is every one that feareth the Lord; that walketh in his ways."

The happiness of which the righteous man will speak has its basis on the premise that the Israelite fears and obeys God. One who attunes himself to God will count as blessings many of the things that an ungodly person takes for granted. Another psalm (Ps. 119) illustrates that even God's laws inspired the psalmist to write one hundred and seventy-six verses of praise and gratitude!

Why will the God-fearing and obedient man be able to appreciate his most basic blessings more than an ungodly person? He will appreciate them more because he will humbly recognize that God made the blessings possible. As implied above, even the law becomes a delight, rather than a burden, to the person who reveres and obeys the Lord.

The righteous man becomes more specific as he illustrates what he has just said. He sets forth the example of a common laborer in the field. Unlike the ungodly man, the righteous laborer does not mind his tiredness. He finds satisfaction in his work (v. 2). Furthermore, he enjoys the fruit of his labor even more, knowing that God has blessed his work.

As the righteous man continues to meditate on the happiness that comes to one who reveres and serves the Lord, his mind turns to his family. A different quality exists in the home that the Lord rules. The worshiper's family flourishes in a spirit of unity. A modern maxim for this joy in family unity is, "The family who prays together stays together."

Even more basic than the blessing of a united family, however, was the blessing of having any family at all. Israelites looked upon children as evidence of God's favor. The righteous man pictured himself as one whom God favored by surrounding him with his own children. The imagery of a wife as a vine and children as olive plants (v. 3) carried deep meaning. The people of Israel prized highly their fruitful vines and olive plants.

In verse 5 the righteous man progressed from thoughts of his immediate family to that of his larger family, the nation. As pointed out earlier, there existed a close unity between the individual and his nation. If the nation failed in some respect, the individual felt a personal responsibility for it.

Conversely, if the nation prospered, the individual felt a personal joy in it. Verse 5 illustrates the righteous man's attitude about the prosperity of Jerusalem. Happy was the man who could witness the prosperity of Jerusalem!

The psalm concludes with the expected rewards of righteousness: longevity and national peace. "Thou shalt see thy children's children, and peace upon Israel!" (v. 6). The saltness of the righteous man would not go unblessed. The Lord would give him the sweet taste of happiness, even in a less than perfect existence.

Earlier we mentioned the fact that the Israelites used Psalm 128 as a "pilgrim song" as they traveled to Jerusalem. Actually, life itself is a pilgrimage. The blessings about which the righteous man sang apply to the whole pilgrimage of life for a God-fearing, obedient person.

Happiness is not so much a matter of what you possess as it is your attitude toward what you possess. Psalm 128 discussed the blessing of work, family, and hope for the nation. In the pilgrimage of life, some persons consider work as pure drudgery; others see even the most menial work as a source of satisfaction. Some persons view family as a burden and a threat to their independence and freedom; others assess family as a profound source of blessing. Some persons, consumed with self-interest, have little concern for the welfare of the nation as a whole. Others show fierce pride in their nation and rejoice in the freedom of all the citizens, not just of the privileged class.

Today, as in the psalmist's day, part of saltness for the upright person is the discovering of a source of God's blessing in all of life's experiences. Unlike the chronic complainer, the God-centered person becomes a positive witness to others through his joyful and thankful outlook on life.

Psalm 84

¹How amiable are thy tabernacles, O Lord of hosts!

²My soul longeth, yea, even fainteth for the courts of the Lord: my heart and my flesh crieth out for the living God.

³Yea, the sparrow hath found an house, and the swallow a nest for herself, where she may lay her young, even thine altars, O Lord of hosts, my King, and my God.

⁴Blessed are they that dwell in thy house: they will be still praising thee. Selah.

. . . .

¹⁰For a day in thy courts is better than a thousand. I had rather be a doorkeeper in the house of my God, than to dwell in the tents of wickedness.

¹¹For the Lord God is a sun and shield: the Lord will give grace and glory: no good thing will he withhold from them that walk uprightly.

¹²O Lord of hosts, blessed is the man that trusteth in thee.

From our studies of Psalms 1 and 128 we have already observed that the righteous man of the Psalter considered himself a person blessed by God. He found happiness in obeying God and meditating upon God's laws. He rejoiced in his work, his family, and the prosperity of his nation. His exuberant joy came alive in the pages of the Psalter.

In a special way, however, this worshiper found happiness in coming to the house of the Lord. Psalm 84 radiates with great feeling his love of the sanctuary and the joy he found in being there. This was probably another "pilgrim song" sung on journeys to Jerusalem.

"How amiable is thy dwelling place, O Lord of hosts!" exclaimed the righteous man. People of today, with churches on so many street corners, scarcely appreciate the awe with which the ancient Israelite viewed the sanctuary. If the building to which the psalmist referred was Solomon's Temple, as scholars believe, it truly was a marvelous sight to behold.

The expression "Thy tabernacles" (KJV) or "dwelling place" (RSV) symbolizes God's constant presence in the sanctuary. The righteous man rejoiced when he could be near God's dwelling place. Psalm 26:8 expresses a similar thought: "Lord, I have loved the habitation of thy house, and the place where thine honour dwelleth."

The righteous man feels the sorrow of being away from God's house just as keenly as he feels the happiness of being present in it. When he cannot be at the sanctuary, he longs to be there (v. 2). He pines away because he wants so much to stand in the Temple courts. His whole being—soul, heart, and flesh—cries out for the living God.

The worshiper's lament leads him to meditate on how blessed the sparrows and swallows are who have nested in the Temple grounds. He actually envies the sparrows for residing so near the sanctuary (v. 3). The psalmist uses the sparrow figure quite differently here than in Psalm 102:7, where he speaks of the loneliness of the sparrow on the housetop.

One thought precipitates another. If the sparrows who nest near the Temple are blessed, the officials who actually reside within the Temple are even more blessed (v. 4).

Happy is the person who has unlimited opportunity, as the priests do, to sing praises to the Lord in the sanctuary.

The righteous man has thought of how blessed the birds and priests are to live in the vicinity of the Temple. In verses 5-9, he comes to the realization that he, too, has cause for happiness, for he is on his way to Zion. If the psalmist meant verse 6 literally, he was referring to a dry valley (Baca) through which the pilgrims had to pass. Even the dry valley, normally dreaded, became a place of springs. If, however, the psalmist used the words figuratively, he may have made reference to the dangers of traveling to Jerusalem from a foreign country. In that case, the dangers of travel would change from hardship to ease. Whether figurative or literal, the verse carries the thought that God will strengthen the worshipers for their journey. This remembrance leads the righteous man to digress briefly and make the spontaneous prayer recorded in verses 8-9.

The worshiper returns to his earlier musing. He would rather spend one day in the Temple courts than a thousand elsewhere (v. 10). As a parallel thought, he adds: "I had rather be a doorkeeper in the house of my God, than to dwell in the tents of wickedness." The point seems to be that he would rather be a humble servant in God's house than a guest in the home of ungodly people.

He closes Psalm 84 with words of praise to the Lord for his protection, favor, and provisions on the journey and elsewhere. Blessed is the man who trusts in the Lord, for the Lord will take care of him.

Happiness was, for the righteous man, being able to go to God's house to worship. His zeal for the Lord and his love of God's house exemplify his saltness in the Israelite community.

Many modern people have become spoiled by the easy availability of our churches. We complain more about too long a worship service or too many different church-related activities than about too brief or too few worship opportunities. We cannot fully appreciate the deep longing of the psalmist to be in God's house.

Nevertheless, times come in the lives of all of us when we get a glimmer of what it feels like not to have the privilege of worshiping in church. Prolonged illness that prevents us from church attendance can help us recognize, negatively, how much our church means to us. Like the psalmist, we may long for an opportunity to return.

A widow, who had no children or other living relatives to help her, literally looked to the church as her family. She attended church every time the doors opened and she gave of herself and substance to the church like a good family member would for his family. She dreaded the times when some of the church activities would be suspended for the summer. This lovely lady's great love for the church approximated that of the psalmist. She found happiness and deep satisfaction in being in God's house.

Righteous people of today, like those of the psalmist's era, assess happiness from a spiritual, rather than material, vantage point. Their example of rejoicing over the right things and in the right way has a preservative effect on society. They become salt in a world where too many people seek happiness in the wrong pursuits and from the wrong sources.

Chapter 2
The Righteous Man
Faces Affliction

Psalm 3

[1]Lord, how are they increased that trouble me! many are they that rise up against me.

[2]Many there be which say of my soul, There is no help for him in God. Selah.

[3]But thou, O Lord, art a shield for me; my glory, and the lifter up of mine head.

[4]I cried unto the Lord with my voice, and he heard me out of his holy hill. Selah.

[5]I laid me down and slept; I awaked; for the Lord sustained me.

[6]I will not be afraid of ten thousands of people, that have set themselves against me round about.

[7]Arise, O Lord; save me, O my God: for thou hast smitten all mine enemies upon the cheek bone; thou hast broken the teeth of the ungodly.

[8]Salvation belongeth unto the Lord: thy blessing is upon thy people. Selah.

In the first chapter of this book, we considered some illustrations of how the righteous man described in the Psalter became "salt" in the way he assessed happiness. In the second section we shall see how the same type of man became a preservative and seasoning example when confronted with affliction. We shall explore Psalms 3, 69, and 10, to learn about this aspect of his saltness. We will begin by examining Psalm 3.

It is one thing to assess happiness a spiritually correct way in prosperous times, as the righteous man did in the preceding psalms. It is another thing altogether to face persecution, affliction, and other troubled times and still retain one's saltness. Psalm 3 brings to mind the godly trust shown by Paul in the Christian era: "Often troubled, but not crushed; sometimes in doubt, but never in despair" (2 Cor. 4:8, TEV).

We have no hard and fast rule by which to determine when the "I" of the psalms represents an individual and when it represents the voice of a whole nation. Likewise, we cannot easily determine when the words of a psalm refer to one specific situation or when they refer to a composite of several situations. Some scholars believe that Psalm 3 refers to afflictions faced by several righteous rulers or to the same ruler on several different occasions. Others believe that Psalm 3 refers to King David's tribulations in the specific incident mentioned in the superscription of the psalm. Neither view detracts from the central idea that God does not allow human schemes to defeat his purposes and that trust in God is a worthy response to all of life's problems.

The title of Psalm 3 indicates that the occasion for the writing of this psalm was King David's flight from his son Absalom. An account from 2 Samuel 15—18 tells of Absalom's attempt to usurp his father's throne through violence, and of Absalom's eventual defeat. If we look for it, we can find in Psalm 3 the evidence of King David's heartbreak because of his son's revolt and of the actual danger in which he found himself. More to the point, however, we see exemplified in the psalm the strength of David's trust in God's providential care.

Psalm 3 takes the form of a lament because of the deep trouble in which the righteous man finds himself. Often, the enemies of the righteous man were foreigners; here, apparently they were his own people. As the psalm opens, the psalmist pours out his troubled heart to God about those who have afflicted him.

"O Lord, how many are my foes! Many are rising against me" (v. 1, RSV), the psalmist complains to God. The conspiracy against him had gained momentum. If the speaker was King David, as some think, he was probably referring to the snowballing growth of rebels led by his son, Absalom. Attack by foreigners hurts badly enough; attack by one's own family members or nation becomes infinitely worse and more difficult to bear. The affliction that had come upon him stunned this righteous man.

As if this distressing plight were not bad enough, he had to listen to the accusing words of those who claimed that he brought it on himself. Verse 2 implies that his fellowmen thought God had punished him for past sins. In that case, he could expect no help from God. In fact, his enemies would have him believe that God had deserted him. This loomed as the most devastating possibility of all.

The psalm seems to come to a crescendo or climax at this point. (The word *selah* directed the instrumentalist to increase the volume while the singers remained silent.) In reading the psalm, we can almost feel the tension building up as the psalmist unfolds the outcome of this crisis situation.

The righteous man refuses to despair! No matter what his enemies think to the contrary, God has not forsaken him. In retrospect, he knows how often God has served as a shield for him in the past when troubles beset him. He refers to the

Lord as his "glory"—a tribute to the fact that since an Israelite king served as God's representative, the king's glory actually came from God. Whether the righteous man was King David or another ruler of Israel, he received his position from God. God had exalted him ("the lifter up of mine head"—v. 3) and given him this status of royalty.

Remembering these past evidences of God's supportive care gave the righteous man confidence to appeal to the Lord again for help. His trust proved well-founded; God listened to his prayer. Again the worshiper emphasizes a high point in the narrative instrumentally with a "Selah" (v. 4).

The effect of the righteous man's renewal of faith must have been great. In spite of the dangers he still faced, he felt so sure of God's protection that he slept without a fear or worry. Although the righteous man knew that his enemies still surrounded him, he no longer feared them, for he and God stood on the same side. The words "smitten . . . upon the cheek bone" (v. 7) express in metaphor a final insult to his enemies when all their resistance had gone. "Broken the teeth of the ungodly" carries the picture of wild beasts who can no longer hurt anyone because their teeth have been broken. These words express the thought that because of God's intervention, these unrighteous enemies would now be powerless.

Psalm 3 ends on the lofty note that God is sufficient to deliver the righteous man in affliction, regardless of how many enemies the man has. Those who trust God and serve him will be delivered and blessed. The righteous man of the psalm is "salt" in the way he faces affliction. He looks for help from the right source, and he trusts the Lord to deliver him.

Affliction in the world of our day can take many forms. It need not take the shape of military revolution, as in the psalmist's case in Psalm 3. Sometimes affliction appears in the form of physical illness, handicaps, broken homes, unjust discrimination, ridicule for one's beliefs, criticism, and poverty. These afflictions can become deadly enemies to our physical, mental, and spiritual well-being if we let them.

Coping with the afflictions of life does not necessarily mean being healed or spared so that the problems no longer exist. It means trusting God to strengthen us so that we can deal constructively with whatever befalls us. "The teeth" of the enemy (regardless of who or what the enemy is) become broken when we trust God to help us. The foe no longer has power over us. Even an enemy like death loses its sting through the victory of faith.

A good modern day example of saltness in the face of affliction is that of a young serviceman who returned from war as a paraplegic. He could have easily turned sour on the world and given up in despair. Instead he chose to ask God's help in becoming a productive human being in spite of his physical plight. The paraplegic man, a deeply committed Christian, now leads a busy life in a very responsible position.

Not all afflicted persons who trust God will end up in lucrative positions. However, they *can* become salt in the community by their continued trust in the Lord despite their afflictions. They can say with the psalmist, "Thou, O Lord, art a shield for me . . . . I will not be afraid of ten thousands of people, that have set themselves against me round about" (Ps. 3:3, 6).

Psalm 69

¹Save me, O God; for the waters are come in unto my soul.

²I sink in deep mire, where there is no standing: I am come into deep waters, where the floods overflow me.

³I am weary of my crying: my throat is dried: mine eyes fail while I wait for my God.

⁴They that hate me without a cause are more than the hairs of mine head: they that would destroy me, being mine enemies wrongfully, are mighty: then I restored that which I took not away.

. . . .

⁶Let not them that wait on thee, O Lord God of hosts, be ashamed for my sake: let not those that seek thee be confounded for my sake, O God of Israel.

. . . .

¹⁶Hear me, O Lord; for thy lovingkindness is good: turn unto me according to the multitude of thy tender mercies.

¹⁷And hide not thy face from thy servant; for I am in trouble: hear me speedily.

. . . .

³⁰I will praise the name of God with a song, and will magnify him with thanksgiving.

. . . .

³²The humble shall see this, and be glad: and your heart shall live that seek God.

³³For the Lord heareth the poor, and despiseth not his prisoners.

Psalm 3 dealt with a stress situation in which the righteous man's own son plotted against him. Psalm 69, our second example of a righteous man facing affliction, deals with enemies outside the family. Both psalms illustrate the righteous man's ability to show a quality of saltness in a difficult situation.

In reading Psalm 69, we can scarcely refrain from comparing the suffering of the man in the psalm with that of Jesus. The unfounded hostility against him and the unjust accusations (v. 4), the shame and reproach (v. 7), the anger he sparked by trying to reform some evil practices in the Temple (v. 9)—these experiences remind us of Jesus. The righteous man's ability to praise God in spite of all his afflictions (vv. 30-36) is also Christlike. However, the comparison must end there. The man in the psalm was not sinless, and he did not share Christ's concept of how enemies should be treated. To the contrary, verses 22-28 clearly show that he desired retaliation. We need to remember, though, that the "eye for an eye" concept was acceptable by Old Testament standards.

Psalm 69 begins with a prayer for deliverance. The Revised Standard Version translates verse 1: "Save me, O God! For the waters have come up to my neck." This picturesque language suggests that the righteous man was in a life-threatening situation. He felt as though he had either sunk in deep mire where he could not find a foothold, or was up to his neck in flood water.

Verse 3 suggests that part of the problem lay in the fact that God had not yet answered his prayer. Facing affliction is hard under any circumstance, but it is especially hard when God seems far away from us. The righteous man had grown weary from the tension of waiting for God to hear his prayer.

In evaluating his situation, the righteous man declares

that the number of his enemies was as great as the number of hairs on his head (v. 4). Without just cause, his enemies wanted to destroy him. They even demanded that he return something he did not steal!

Because of the righteous man's religious zeal, many of those in the community of faith had looked up to him as an example. He feared that if God did not vindicate him, he would become a source of shame or stumbling block to them. His reasoning was probably based on the concept that the righteous person is protected and defended by God.

Verses 9-12 provide some insight as to the reason the man's enemies hated him. He evidently had attempted some reforms in the Temple that his enemies did not like. Verse 9 speaks of his being eaten up with zeal for the Lord. He felt such great anguish over the insults hurled against the Lord that he wore mourning clothes to show his penitence for what his countrymen had done.

Considering the extremity of his plight, the righteous man's plea in verse 16 seems reasonable. He knows of the Lord's steadfast love and mercy and asks that it be extended to him. He longs to feel God's presence and to experience his deliverance from this present trouble. He describes himself as being brokenhearted over the complete lack of compassion shown him by his fellowman. Figuratively, he says that when he asked for food, he received gall (a bitter poison). When he asked for something to quench his thirst, he received vinegar (v. 21).

Temporarily, the worshiper's resentment went out of control. Verses 22-28 illustrate the intensity of the bitterness that had built up within him. He wanted God to punish his enemies unmercifully. In this respect, he reflected the accepted customs and the degree of spiritual immaturity of the people of his day. The worshiper's desire for revenge runs completely contrary to Christian principles. Nevertheless, the ancient worshiper would justify such a desire as fitting in with God's practice of punishing evil and rewarding goodness.

After working his way through his bitterness about his plight, the righteous man once more emerges as a thankful worshiper (v. 30). His whole tone changes as he sings his hymn of gratitude to the Lord. In contrast to his earlier conduct, he now resumes his basically righteous stance. In saying that the Lord desires thanksgiving more than animal sacrifice, he shows unusual moral perception for his day. Furthermore, he now recognizes that God's scale of justice will be balanced after all. The Lord really does hear the poor and the afflicted (v. 33).

The psalm ends with a call to all creation to praise the Lord. The righteous man has confidence that with God's help, his own future and that of his nation will be secure. "God will save Zion ... and they that love his name shall dwell therein" (vv. 35-36).

After studying the psalm, you may wonder why we included Psalm 69 in the section on "A Righteous Man Faces Affliction," especially in view of the vindictive statements of verses 22-27. Primarily, we did it for two reasons. (1) Psalm 69 illustrates the worshiper's trust in the power of God to deliver him from his troubled plight. The righteous man shows his saltness in his confidence that God will act justly and in his thankfulness to God for doing so. (2) The psalm illustrates the fact that even a basically righteous man can face dark trials of faith in which he feels temporarily forsaken. Just as a person must work through a period of grief after bereavement, so must he often work through a period of bitterness and resentment in times of personal affliction. A person's saltness is manifest when he can overcome bitterness about his lot and can still praise God.

There are times when most of us feel that we are "neck-deep" in troubles, as the psalmist expressed it in verse 1. We feel overwhelmed by the opposition we are meeting or the problems we are facing. We find that we must endure a lonely, depressing experience.

Our first impulse may be a noble one—to call on God for help and to listen and wait for his answer. God does not always give an instant answer, however, and so we become impatient. We want immediate assurance that God will soon deliver us from our present troubles.

Our second impulse is less noble than our first one. Like the psalmist, we lash out against those who have wronged us. Even though we know that bitterness and revenge run contrary to Christ's teachings, we find them hard to resist.

Our third impulse, as basically righteous people, comes after we work through our anger and frustration. We suddenly realize that God has not been deaf to our prayers after all. He has been there all along, quietly strengthening us and helping us. We feel like singing out so that the whole world may hear: Thank you, Lord! Thank you!

Saltness does not mean refusing to admit to self or to other people that we have problems or that we have been hurt. Trouble is an accepted fact of life for most people in the present world. Saltness involves working through our problems with God's help, then emerging with a victorious faith. With the psalmist, we can then say: "I will praise the name of God with a song, and will magnify him with thanksgiving" (Ps. 69:30).

Psalm 10

¹Why standest thou afar off, O Lord? Why hidest thou thyself in times of trouble?

²The wicked in his pride doth persecute the poor: let them be taken in the devices that they have imagined.

. . . .

⁵His ways are always grievous; thy judgments are far above out of his sight: as for all his enemies, he puffeth at them.

. . . .

⁷His mouth is full of cursing and deceit and fraud: under his tongue is mischief and vanity.

⁸He sitteth in the lurking places of the villages: in the secret places doth he murder the innocent: his eyes are privily set against the poor.

. . . .

¹¹He hath said in his heart, God hath forgotten: he hideth his face; he will never see it.

¹²Arise, O Lord; O God, lift up thine hand: forget not the humble.

. . . .

¹⁷Lord, thou hast heard the desire of the humble: thou wilt prepare their heart, thou wilt cause thine ear to hear:

¹⁸To judge the fatherless and the oppressed, that the man of the earth may no more oppress.

The apparent prosperity of the wicked and the affliction of the righteous is a lament theme throughout the Psalter and much of the rest of the Old Testament. The section on "A Righteous Man Faces Affliction" would be incomplete without a reference to this problem. Psalm 10 serves to illustrate the perplexity of the worshiper as he tries to cope with it.

Because of their similarity in structure, most scholars believe that Psalms 9 and 10 originally stood as one psalm. However, the tone of the two psalms differs considerably. Psalm 9 is a thanksgiving hymn, whereas Psalm 10 is a lament. We can easily see why a compiler might later divide the two hymns. Psalm 10 probably came into use in the ancient ritual ceremonies celebrating God as king.

As already indicated, Psalm 10 has as its theme the seeming injustices of the world. The righteous man reveals his saltness as he discovers that things are not always what they appear to be. The psalm concludes with a testimony that the Lord indeed loves justice and cares what happens to those who serve him.

Psalm 10 begins with a question that evidently puzzled ancient worshipers many times. Why did God seem to do nothing to help his worshipers in their hours of affliction? (v. 1). Did he not care that those who loved and obeyed him had received cruel treatment? At other times God had made his presence and nearness felt very plainly (Ps. 33:18; 75:1), but at that moment God seemed far off.

The righteous man reviews what has happened. He decries that "in arrogance the wicked hotly pursue the poor" (v. 2, RSV). He wishes that the wicked would get caught in their own traps.

In verses 3-7, the worshiper describes the character of those who tyrannize the poor and the humble. These evil people are greedy and covetous (v. 3). They are atheistic in their outlook (v. 4). They appear secure in their own conceits, not giving any thought to the possibility of God pun-

ishing them or of anything bad happening to them (vv. 5-6).
They sin verbally by cursing, lying, and speaking oppres-
sively (v. 7). And these words only describe the *character* of
the evil people! The description of the wicked men's *conduct* follows in verses 8-11.

The evil persons of whom the righteous man speaks lie in
ambush, waiting to murder innocent people, especially the
poor (v. 8). These wicked men think that God will not inter-
fere or that he will pretend not to know what is going on
(v. 11).

The unwritten question in this psalm is, Why be righteous
if God does not reward righteousness or punish wickedness? Verses 12-16 seem to bear out this thought. The righteous man appeals to God to prove that he (God) is not
indifferent by vindicating the righteous and punishing the
wicked. He puzzles over why God has continued to tolerate
the blasphemy of these evil people for this long. He fears
that God's inaction has led them to think that they will not
be held accountable for their profane conduct (v. 13).

Suddenly the righteous man reawakens to the truth that
he has temporarily overlooked an important fact. In spite of
outward appearances to the contrary, the Lord is not blind
to what happens to his people. He has a keen awareness of
the evil that has gone on and about the suffering it has
caused his faithful worshiper. In his own time and way, he
will deal with it. God does not desert the poor and the help-
less who have committed themselves to his care. The worshiper now anticipates the time when God will render the
evil man powerless and will find no more wickedness in the
land (vv. 14-15).

The doubts that the righteous man formerly experienced
because of his oppression have now been resolved.
Through the eyes of faith he can once again see that God
still rules over the world and that his oppressors will not be

victorious after all (v. 16). He concludes his lament psalm with a prayer of thanksgiving to God for listening to him and upholding the cause of justice and righteousness.

Saltness for the righteous man of the Psalter did not come easily when he had to face affliction. It never does, under those circumstances. Seeing life and religion in proper perspective is very difficult for a person facing persecution and oppression.

Before the righteous man could become "salt," he had to rise above the doubts and fears that plagued his finite mind and commit himself, in faith, to God's care. He had to recognize that things are not always what they appear to be. The prosperity of the wicked will not last forever. God, in his infinite wisdom, will balance the scales of justice at his own appointed time. Until then, impatience for justice must be tempered with patient faith and the sure knowledge that God hears the prayers of his people.

In some respects, human nature has not changed much through the centuries. Worshipers of today still have to wrestle with the question of why God sometimes permits ungodly people to prosper while righteous people must struggle. This question cannot easily be resolved.

For the Christian, saltness in times of trouble involves being able to say: "Lord, I don't quite understand why you allow these things to happen, but I do know that you still control the world. Strengthen my faith so that I can wait more patiently for your scale of justice to balance." The example of this kind of faith inspires others within the community of believers to wait more patiently also.

Chapter 3
The Righteous Man Exults in Faith

Psalm 23

[1]The Lord is my shepherd; I shall not want.

[2]He maketh me to lie down in green pastures: he leadeth me beside the still waters.

[3]He restoreth my soul: he leadeth me in the paths of righteousness for his name's sake.

[4]Yea, though I walk through the valley of the shadow of death, I will fear no evil: for thou art with me; thy rod and thy staff they comfort me.

[5]Thou preparest a table before me in the presence of mine enemies: thou anointest my head with oil; my cup runneth over.

[6]Surely goodness and mercy shall follow me all the days of my life: and I will dwell in the house of the Lord for ever.

Of all the ways in which the righteous man of the Psalter became salt to his own generation, his demonstration of confident faith was most moving. We could cite many psalms to illustrate the faith of the righteous man, but only three have been chosen for this discussion. Psalm 23 shows the worshiper's concept of God as the good shepherd and the gracious host, Psalm 46 as the secure shelter and hiding place, and Psalm 27 as the dispeller of fear and giver of light.

The twenty-third Psalm is unquestionably the most widely used one in the Psalter by Christians of today. It has brought comfort and inspiration to many people because of its expressions of sure faith that relate to a lifetime of experiences. Whether in times of sorrow, meditation, or uncertainty, Psalm 23 has a message of optimism and trust that undergirds each believer's own faith.

Psalm 23 begins with the simple statement of faith, "The Lord is my shepherd." The Old Testament frequently uses the shepherd image. For example, Isaiah 40:11 speaks of God as tending his flock like a shepherd. Isaiah 63:14 describes the careful way God leads his people to prevent them from stumbling. Ezekiel tells of God's rescue of his sheep from those who would devour them. However, the prophets generally used the shepherd image on a national level, whereas the psalmist used it on the individual level.

The righteous man of the Psalter had a personal awareness of God's shepherding influence on his life. The Lord had not left him to wander aimlessly and unprotected. Like a conscientious shepherd, God had led him.

In the day of the psalmist, a shepherd had to account strictly for each sheep in the flock that he herded. If he allowed one to stray and get lost, he had to find it. If he saw one in danger of being attacked, he had to try to protect it. If he could not save a sheep from being ravaged, he had to bring proof to the owner of the flock that the sheep could not have been saved. A truly devoted shepherd might even willingly lay down his life for his sheep. Moreover, a good shepherd's motivation came not only from his accountability to the owner, but also his personal concern for the sheep.

The righteous man of the Psalter sees in the Lord some of the same attributes seen in a good shepherd. However, since the Lord both owns and shepherds his flock, he cannot be held accountable to another. The Lord's motivation, therefore, lies strictly in the love and concern he has for his flock. The righteous man recognizes the care that God gives, and he openly acknowledges it.

The saltness of the righteous man becomes apparent in the confident trust he has that God will continue to watch over him. He says with assurance, "I shall not want" (v. 1). Although he expresses his personal trust here, he may be remembering also how God met the needs of the Israelites during their wilderness wandering. On both an individual and national level, God had provided for his people. Furthermore, the righteous man had confidence that God would continue to do it in the future. Just as the ancient Israelite viewed the mind, body, and soul as an entity of inseparable parts of the whole person, so he saw the past, present, and future as a continuous chain of human existence. He regarded the Lord as a consistent God, not a capricious one. The God who had shown his concern for his people in the past and present would continue to do it in the future. Thus, the righteous man can say confidently, "I shall not want" (be lacking).

Continuing with the figure of a shepherd, verse 2 illustrates the Lord's compassionate care. Shepherds tried to lead the flock to cool green pastures near water where they could rest and be refreshed during the heat of the day. The Lord served as this kind of shepherd: a guiding, caring, sustaining one.

The ancient Israelites viewed the human soul as the vitalizing force in life that holds the person together and gives him the power to keep going. The righteous man of Psalm 23 experienced not only the sustaining power of the Lord, but also the actual renewal of vitality ("He restoreth my soul"—v. 3). God's name, Yahweh, means "I am who I am" (Ex. 3:14, RSV). It refers to God's presence and action throughout history. In Psalm 23:3, the righteous man pictures the Lord as one who is true to his name. The eternally righteous God, who played so great a part in history, would be out of character if he did not lead his flock in the paths of righteousness.

Life, whether for sheep or for humans, has its dark times. Those dark places become infinitely easier to cope with when we are in the company of someone we trust. Just as the shepherd protects his sheep with his rod (a club used for defense) and his staff (that which gives support in the slippery places), so the Lord stays close to and strengthens his people to give them comfort in the hard places. Experiencing the Lord's presence with us (v. 4) strengthens us. The words "valley of the shadow of death" can more accurately be translated "valley of deep darkness." A very real valley of darkness for sheep would be a place where other beasts could easily attack the sheep. Likewise, for humans the threat of death, whether of self or loved ones, becomes a dark valley. However, death is not the only ravine of deep darkness; pain, loneliness, betrayal, and failure are dark places, too. In all these places, and with the memory of past affliction still lingering in his mind, the righteous man of the Psalter could still say with confidence, "I am not afraid."

In verse 5 the imagery of the psalm changes from shepherd to host. Not only had the Lord been a good shepherd; he had also been a good host. In ancient days a host assumed responsibility for the safety of the guests for as long as the guests remained. This duty included protection from enemies who might lurk outside. In addition, the host did everything he could for the pleasure of the guests, including anointing the heads of the guests with perfumed oil and preparing a sumptuous banquet for them. In retrospect the righteous man realized that this function was exactly what the Lord had performed for him. The Lord was, and is, and will be a gracious host to his people, protecting, sustaining, and fulfilling them. The Lord does more than enough to satisfy the needs of the righteous man. The worshiper's cup overflows.

By inference, the righteous man may have been thinking how the fate of the ungodly person contrasted to his own fate. Psalm 1 and other psalms dwell on this thought. More to the point, however, his confident hope enabled him to look forward to evidences of God's goodness and mercy for the rest of his life. Whether through his corporate worship experiences or in his daily walk of life, the righteous man could anticipate intimate fellowship with God (v. 6).

Because of its reference to the valley of the shadow of death, Psalm 23 has become a standard funeral Scripture, almost to the exclusion of its use elsewhere. This is unfortunate, even though it does bring comfort to mourners. Actually, the psalmist wrote it as an expression of joyous trust in the Lord for the "here and now" rather than the hereafter. Psalm 23 is a hymn to *live* by, a confident testimony of certainty in this world of uncertainty.

Confrontation with danger and sorrow is a part of life, but not the only part. The Good Shepherd who leads us safely through the dark places also leads us through the green pastures. If we expect him to shepherd us at death, we must begin by trusting him to shepherd us in life.

The Lord continues to be both a conscientious shepherd and a good host to his people. He provides for our needs. He leads us in straight paths. He restores our vitality. He protects and comforts us so that we need not be afraid. He anoints us with honor and gives us a life that overflows with blessings. With the Lord as our host, we shall continue to experience his goodness and mercy throughout life.

The exulting kind of faith shown by the psalmist in Psalm 23 provides us with a good pattern to follow today. Like this worshiper of old, we can live out a testimony of faith. Saltness for the Christian, as for the psalmist, involves retaining one's savor whether going through green pastures or dark valleys.

Psalm 46

[1]God is our refuge and strength, a very present help in trouble.

[2]Therefore will not we fear, though the earth be removed, and though the mountains be carried into the midst of the sea;

[3]Though the waters thereof roar and be troubled, though the mountains shake with the swelling thereof. Selah.

[4]There is a river, the streams whereof shall make glad the city of God, the holy place of the tabernacles of the most High.

[5]God is in the midst of her; she shall not be moved: God shall help her, and that right early.

. . . .

[7]The Lord of hosts is with us; the God of Jacob is our refuge. Selah.

. . . .

⁹He maketh wars to cease unto the end of the earth; he breaketh the bow, and cutteth the spear in sunder; he burneth the chariot in the fire.

¹⁰Be still, and know that I am God: I will be exalted among the heathen, I will be exalted in the earth.

¹¹The Lord of hosts is with us; the God of Jacob is our refuge. Selah.

Psalm 46 has been called one of the most powerful testimonies of faith and poetry of the Old Testament. The expressive beauty of the psalm is surpassed only by the quality of faith it illustrates.

Scholars have offered various explanations as to what prompted the writing of Psalm 46. Some of them believe that the psalm refers to a specific historical crisis, such as the deliverance of Jerusalem from Sennacherib's army. Others believe that it combined historical events, or that the psalmist wrote it for a special Israelite festival. Whatever the crisis or occasion that inspired it, Psalm 46 expresses in a moving way the faith of a righteous man whose words still lift and inspire the hearts of worshipers today.

Speaking as a representative of all true worshipers, the righteous man begins his testimony with a stirring expression of faith: "God is our refuge and strength, a very present help in trouble" (v. 1). In both the past and present, God has proved himself to be a haven of protection and a strong fortress for his people. With the Lord to protect him, the worshiper had no need to turn to other sources for his strength. He had a secure awareness of God's constant presence to help him, regardless of the kind of trouble in which he found himself.

Like most perceptive persons, the righteous man viewed the creation of the world and the powerful forces of nature as awesome. The changing earth, the tottering mountains, and the roaring water would strike awe in the heart of any person. For the worshiper, the awe remained what it was, however—a reverent regard for the works of God's hands, not a source of terror. Faith enabled the righteous man to say that he would not fear the forces of nature, no matter what happened (vv. 2-3). He based his statement on the fact that he trusted God, his refuge and strength, to take care of him.

In verse 4, the righteous man picks up a metaphor that would communicate instantly to an Israelite. The Israelites valued few things as much as they did a river. Rivers represented fertility for the land. Without rivers, the crops and livestock would perish. Any land that had many rivers was considered prosperous. Rivers also figuratively represented power, as in the case of Assyria's abundant rivers.

Jerusalem had become known as the "City of God" because of its establishment as a worship center. The people, therefore, thought of God as dwelling there. In verses 4-5, the righteous man pictures God as a life-giving river running throughout the city, a stream that brings gladness to all its inhabitants. Isaiah 33:21 uses a similar figure to describe God's presence. The Lord is always there, ready to help Israel. With God in her midst, Israel has nothing to fear.

Continuing in a spirit of confident trust, the righteous man considers the Lord's presence from another perspective. Not only did God bring gladness to Israel, he also became a source of great power in Israel's behalf. The worshiper recalls how other nations ("heathens," v. 6) roared and tottered, but all that the Lord had to do was speak and the whole earth would melt. No matter what battle Israel had to fight, the worshiper could say with assurance: "The Lord of hosts is with us; the God of Jacob is our refuge" (v. 7).

The righteous man's testimony in verse 7 had a firm basis. The events of Israel's history had already proved what the Lord can do. As the need arose, the Lord could destroy Israel's enemies, delivering Israel in times of war. However, the Lord could also bring an end to wars on earth. The righteous man used the expressions "breaketh the bow . . . burneth the chariot" (v. 9) as figures of speech to describe God's ability to bring peace.

Seen in this context, the familiar words of verse 10 ("Be still, and know that I am God") take on added meaning. Loosely paraphrased, the quotation attributed to the Lord says: "Quit roaring in a warlike manner and recognize that I am God. *I* (not you) will be exalted in the earth." Israel's God is also the universal God and his kingdom is one of peace, not war.

The worshiper pictures the crisis as now being over. The salty man of the Psalms concludes his testimony of faith with a confident refrain that all Israel can join him in singing: "The Lord of hosts is with us; the God of Jacob is our refuge" (v. 11).

In recent years America has gone through many crises: energy shortages, unstable economy, unemployment problems, international crises, and so forth. "Roaring" has been heard from all sides—from outraged motorists, striking workers, worried homemakers, critical economists, and angry politicians. Maybe all of us need to stop roaring long enough to hear the message of Psalm 46: "Be still, and know that I am God: *I* will be exalted" (v. 10).

We have exalted just about everything except God, and much of what we have exalted has failed. We believed that we had an unlimited amount of fuel energy, but we learned that we do not. We counted on so-called "cost of living" raises to take care of the demands of an inflated economy, but they have not. Could the problem be that instead of exalting God, we have exalted our own self-interests for so long that we are merely reaping the results of our own sins?

The time is more than ripe for us to trust and exalt the Lord instead of trusting and exalting things. Only then can we hope to discover what the psalmist learned so long ago: "God is our refuge and strength, a very present help in trouble" (Ps. 46:1).

Psalm 27

¹The Lord is my light and my salvation; whom shall I fear? the Lord is the strength of my life; of whom shall I be afraid?

²When the wicked, even mine enemies and my foes, came upon me to eat up my flesh, they stumbled and fell.

³Though an host should encamp against me, my heart shall not fear: though war should rise against me, in this will I be confident.

⁴One thing have I desired of the Lord, that will I seek after; that I may dwell in the house of the Lord all the days of my life, to behold the beauty of the Lord, and to enquire in his temple.

⁵For in the time of trouble he shall hide me in his pavilion: in the secret of his tabernacle shall he hide me; he shall set me up upon a rock.

⁶And now shall mine head be lifted up

above mine enemies round about me: therefore will I offer in his tabernacle sacrifices of joy; I will sing, yea, I will sing praises unto the Lord.

In this section on "The Righteous Man Exults in Faith" we have already discussed two examples. Psalm 23, a psalm precious to people through the ages because of its beautiful imagery, focused on the worshiper's trust in the Lord as his Shepherd and host. Psalm 46 emphasized the worshiper's testimony of faith in God's protective power and the need for all mankind to be still long enough to recognize the universal lordship of God. The third psalm in this section shows the worshiper's faith in God as the light of his life and the dispeller of his fears. All three psalms illustrate the saltness of the righteous man as he set a personal example of faith for the community of true worshipers to follow.

Psalm 27 really comprises two separate psalms. Verses 1-6 form a song of trust, whereas verses 7-14 form a lament. For this reason, we shall only deal with the first six verses of the psalm here. Apparently Psalm 27:1-6 relates to a time of trouble in the life of the psalmist. It focuses on the way the worshiper's victorious faith enabled him to cope with the forces that threatened his life.

As in Psalm 46, the righteous man begins his testimony in Psalm 27 with an expression of faith. He declares: "The Lord is my light and my salvation; whom shall I fear? the Lord is the strength of my life; of whom shall I be afraid?" (v. 1). The figure of light, as used in the Psalter, conveys several ideas. It illuminates the dark places of life (4:6). It brings pleasure and joy (97:11). It is the source of life (36:9). The righteous man may have had all three meanings in mind when he spoke of the Lord as his light.

He also views the Lord as his salvation. A verse from the "Song of Moses" in Exodus 15:2 speaks in a similar fashion of the Lord as being "my salvation." The term, as used here, refers to deliverance, especially from the hands of the enemy.

The righteous man meditates on what it means to have the Lord as his light, his salvation, and the strength of his life. He concludes that with the Lord to lighten his way, deliver him, and be his stronghold, he has nothing to fear. He has confident trust that the Lord can meet his needs in every circumstance of life.

As the righteous man considers one of the problem areas of his life (his foes), he feels convinced that the Lord will prove to be a trustworthy deliverer. The expression "eat up my flesh" (v. 2) is a metaphor that conveys the idea that his enemies were like wild beasts, waiting to eat him up. Instead of devouring him as they had planned, however, his enemies find themselves stumbling and falling. In fact, so confident does the righteous man become of the Lord's help that he will not fear, even if a whole army rises against him (v. 3).

Many persons, paralyzed by the fear of what might happen to them, seem unable to relax and to enter into an experience of worship. The righteous man did not have that problem. Freed from fear because of his trust in the Lord, he could concentrate on more spiritual goals. His petition in verse 4 points toward one of the goals: that he may always continue to be in the house of the Lord and to ask God's guidance while he dwells there. In other words, his utmost desire was to bask in the serene beauty of the Temple and to commune with God continuously.

Verse 5 again suggests the imagery of God as a gracious host, a figure that we found in the twenty-third Psalm. As explained in the discussion of Psalm 23, in Old Testament times a good host had a sacred obligation to protect any guest in his home. If an enemy tried to attack the guest, the host protected and defended the guest with his very life. In verse 5 the righteous man laid claim on that promise. The Lord served as gracious host of the tabernacle (his house). The worshiper could count on the Lord to protect and hide him in times of trouble. Whether the enemy was a human being or something intangible, it would be dealt with by God. The Lord would set his guest safely on a high rock. Indeed, the "rock" to which the psalmist referred was God himself, a name that the psalmist applied to the Lord many times (for example, Ps. 18:2; 92:15; 31:3; 61:2; 95:1).

The victorious faith of the righteous man enabled him to be secure, even in the presence of his enemies ("and now shall mine head be lifted up," v. 6). His heart overflowing with gratitude, the worshiper now offers his sacrifice of joy and his song of praise.

The salt of the righteous man, as revealed in Psalm 27, expressed itself in two realms: (1) the faith to trust God in all of the circumstances of life; and (2) the ability to become a seasoning influence among the covenant people through his spirit of true worship. The example of this worshiper offers a challenge for true worshipers of every generation to imitate.

We who are called "Christians" have Christ as our final authority on what it means to exult in faith in all the experiences of life. The Beatitudes exemplify how Christians can have an outlook of courageous faith in difficult circumstances. Christ's personal example and the one set by his apostles in the days of early Christianity illustrate what it means to face the future with faith.

A man who had gone through the trauma of a serious heart attack received this bit of advice from a counselor: "If you want to avoid having another heart attack, you are going to have to stop worrying and start facing life calmly. If you believe in God like you say you do, prove it by trusting him instead of facing life scared. Excessive worrying will only dig you an early grave."

The man took the counselor at his word. He became more relaxed and began to savor life more than ever before, but that was only part of the story. He has begun to trust the Lord more now than ever before. He has learned what it means to exult in faith.

If the righteous man of the Psalter, unblessed by the knowledge of the gospel, could say "The Lord is the strength of my life; of whom shall I be afraid?" how much more should Christians be able to do it! Like the heart attack victim, we may need to learn what trusting the Lord really means.

Chapter 4
The Righteous Man
Copes with Doubt

Psalm 77

¹I cried unto God with my voice, even unto God with my voice; and he gave ear unto me.

²In the day of my trouble I sought the Lord: my sore ran in the night, and ceased not: my soul refused to be comforted.

³I remembered God, and was troubled: I complained, and my spirit was overwhelmed. Selah.

⁴Thou holdest mine eyes waking: I am so troubled that I cannot speak.

. . . .

⁹Hath God forgotten to be gracious? hath he in anger shut up his tender mercies? Selah.

. . . .

¹¹I will remember the works of the Lord: surely I will remember thy wonders of old.

. . . .

¹⁴Thou art the God that doest wonders: thou hast declared thy strength among the people.

. . . .

¹⁹Thy way is in the sea, and thy path in the great waters, and thy footsteps are not known.

There comes a time in the life of nearly every believer, regardless of how righteous the person is, when doubt temporarily clouds faith. Matters which go unquestioned in the good times of life may become objects of uncertainty in times of stress. Questions arise in the mind of the troubled believer, such as: Does God really care what happens to me? Why doesn't God intervene? Why doesn't God at least provide me with some sign which will serve as reassurance? These are important questions that are not easily resolved. They can become, in effect, a trial of our faith.

The "salt of the earth" (Christ's disciples) experienced their share of doubts and fears. During Christ's ministry, he had to rebuke his disciples from time to time about their wavering faith. Nevertheless, the growth and continuation of Christianity shows that with God's help the followers of Christ have successfully coped with doubt and become, as their name "salt" implies, a preserving and seasoning influence in society.

The psalmist evidently had to cope with many times of doubt during his lifetime. We shall discuss some examples of his confrontation with doubt in this section of the book, using Psalms 77, 22, and 13 as illustrations. Unlike Christ's disciples, the psalmist did not have Christ's presence to strengthen his faith. However, he did have a knowledge of God's great acts in the past and a revelation through nature of God's power and grace in the present. These assets helped him to cope victoriously with doubt and to serve as salt in his own community.

Psalm 77 contains a good example of the appearance of doubt in the life of an otherwise righteous man. So closely does this psalm resemble Habakkuk's cry at a time of national defeat, and especially his prayer in the third chapter of the book, that the psalmist almost sounds as if he were Habakkuk or vice versa. In any event, a time of national exile may well have been the background of Psalm 77.

The psalmist begins Psalm 77 by expressing the dilemma of the righteous man. Following his usual custom, the righteous man had addressed himself to God in prayer for an answer to a distressing situation, either a national exile or a personal problem. Day and night he had stretched forth his hands in prayer, yet he found no relief or reassurance. His soul refused to be comforted.

Verse 3 seems to indicate that the righteous man normally felt inspired and strengthened when he meditated about God. Now, however, he found himself grieving when he thought of God. He was worrying so much about his problem that he found he could not sleep. He even had trouble speaking rationally (v. 4).

During those sleepless nights, the righteous man dwells on the way things used to be between God and his people. In years past, God had shown great mercy; why not now? He keeps searching for an answer, but no answer comes. His deepest concern relates to two fears. First, he fears that God has permanently withdrawn his favor from his people. Second, he fears that the Lord has changed character and shall no longer be the gracious God he used to be. The man temporarily experiences grave doubt.

The whole tone of the psalm changes in verse 11. The scales of doubt seem to fall from the psalmist's eyes, allowing him to view the situation from a new perspective. He now sees the matter as it really is. The problem lay in him, not in God. In his anxiety the righteous man had tried to fit God into the mold of man and to exact an answer according to human specifications. He failed to take account of the fact that God cannot be bound by the structured plans of man.

This new perspective enabled the righteous man to move not only from doubt to faith, but also from complaint to praise (vv. 11-15). In retrospect he considers what God did for his people in the past, especially in redeeming Israel so wondrously. How could he have doubted when he knew from past experience and from history what a merciful and great God the Lord had proved himself to be?

The righteous man discovers that nature recognized in the Creator what the righteous man had temporarily overlooked (vv. 16-18). While the righteous man busied himself with doubts and complaints, nature had borne witness to the awesome works of God. The waters revered him; the powers of the sky obeyed him; the earth trembled in recognition of him.

In history and in nature the righteous man made an important discovery. The fact that God does not noisily march through history does not mean that God is not present or active. Sometimes God leads quietly and accomplishes his purpose without fanfare, causing his footsteps to go unrecognized (v. 19). In just such a manner, God had led his people gently through the wilderness. The fact that Israel either forgot or doubted God's presence and participation in the nation's life did not mean that God was not present. God had gone with them each step of the way.

In like manner the Lord had been with the righteous man in his time of trouble, but the man just had not recognized it. His renewed faith enabled this basically good man to work through his doubt and to trust the Lord, even in bleak times.

He knew now that God's gracious character had not changed after all. The compassionate Lord of history still cared about his people.

The saltness of the righteous man of Psalm 77 was restored as he recognized God's gracious hand in history. He had also come to a new awareness of God's leading in his own life. The crucial point of the psalm was not the appearance of doubt in a life of faith, but the way the righteous man coped with doubt when it came.

Temporary doubt sometimes comes into the lives of basically righteous persons of today because of a devastating experience. This kind of doubt need not produce permanent spiritual damage. The key to coping successfully with doubt in troubled times is to keep searching for God's answer while you continue to work through your doubt. In other words, try not to get "hung up" either on self-pity or doubt; otherwise, you won't progress beyond the doubting stage.

A seminary student lost his vision for about a year as a result of an accident. He reacted at first in a spirit of rebellion. He wrestled with the questions, How can I pursue my studies without vision? Why did God call me into the ministry, then allow this accident to occur?

The seminary student learned a lot about life and faith as he worked his way through the dark period of doubt and blindness. With the help of his roommate and the strength that God provides, he continued to pursue his studies. He passed his courses with high honors, but through the blindness he learned a lot more than through the lectures. He learned in a personal way the difference between tested and untested faith.

Misfortune often occurs as a result of human error, not God's direct will. At times, however, God does permit us to go through dark hours in order to test and strengthen our faith. The salty Christian is the one who becomes victorious over doubt, even when his faith has been severely tested.

Psalm 22

¹My God, my God, why hast thou forsaken me? why art thou so far from helping me, and from the words of my roaring?

²O my God, I cry in the daytime, but thou hearest not; and in the night season, and am not silent.

. . . .

⁶But I am a worm, and no man; a reproach of men, and despised of the people.

. . . .

¹⁴I am poured out like water, and all my bones are out of joint: my heart is like wax; it is melted in the midst of my bowels.

¹⁵My strength is dried up like a potsherd; and my tongue cleaveth to my jaws; and thou hast brought me into the dust of death.

. . . .

¹⁹But be not thou far from me, O Lord: O my strength, haste thee to help me.

. . . .

²²I will declare thy name unto my brethren: in the midst of the congregation will I praise thee.

. . . .

**²⁴For he hath not despised nor abhorred
the affliction of the afflicted; neither hath
he hid his face from him; but when he cried
unto him, he heard.**

The opening words of Psalm 22 immediately bring to
mind Jesus' own agonizing cry on the cross. The words of
Jesus in Matthew 27:46 came from this psalm. It is not sur-
prising, therefore, that we connect Psalm 22 with the later
crucifixion of Jesus. However, we can also appropriately
apply Psalm 22 to righteous people of any generation. For
example, Jews might apply the psalm to Israel as a whole,
or to David, Jeremiah, or any other religiously upright person who had undergone suffering. As noted in the study of
the other two psalms in this section, even otherwise righteous persons can experience religious doubts in times of
extreme mental and physical anguish.

In studying the above representative verses from Psalm
22, you will notice that Psalms 77, 13, and 22 reach the
same conclusion. The conclusion is that of confident hope
for the future in spite of present suffering. In each case, the
saltness of the righteous man becomes evident in his open
testimony of faith, arrived at after struggling through experiences of loneliness and doubt.

Nothing could devastate an ancient Israelite more than
the thought that God had forsaken him. The opening words
of verse 1 convey deep feelings of grief: "My God, my God,
why hast thou forsaken me?" The remaining words of verse
1, and the verses that follow, tell us why the righteous man
thought that God had forsaken him.

The righteous man had gone through a period of extreme loneliness and suffering. His words in the first verse
were not a criticism of God, but rather a searching for the

answer to a perplexing question of faith. Why would God appear to leave him helplessly alone to face affliction? Why would he remove himself from the cries ("roaring") of a faithful worshiper? Day and night the righteous man had cried, yet God had not spoken to him (v. 2).

Temporarily, in verses 3-5, the righteous man's thoughts drift to his forefathers who trusted God and received deliverance. Quickly, however, his thoughts return to his own situation. He pictures himself as a worm, trampled underfoot by those who despise him (v. 6). His enemies scornfully cry out that if God really delighted in the worshiper, he would deliver him.

Verses 14-15 portray the effect of the righteous man's mental anguish on his physical health. "I am poured out like water" (v. 14) means figuratively that his "life sap" or strength was gone. The bones of his limbs will not support him. His heart is like melted wax, and his mouth feels so dry that his tongue cleaves to his jaw. He thinks that God wants him to die and return to dust. Verse 18, like verse 1, brings to mind the crucifixion of Jesus that occurred centuries later. The immediate meaning in Psalm 22 is figurative, however. In verse 16 the righteous man had described his enemies as "dogs." Therefore, "they pierced my hands and feet" (v. 16) probably continues the dog-figure used earlier in the verse. It means that his foes nipped ("pierced") him like dogs. Verse 18 ("They part my garments among them, and cast lots") refers to the fact that his foes already anticipated his death and were waiting to divide his garments. Both the piercing of hands and feet and the parting of garments found ultimate fulfilment later at Christ's crucifixion.

The righteous man has reached the end of his own resources. His own strength alone has proved insufficient. With great urgency he calls upon the Lord to help him (v. 19).

God, in his omnipotence, does for the worshiper what the

worshiper cannot do for himself. The Lord lifts the righteous man from cries of agonized doubt to exclamations of joy. Clearly, the righteous man recognizes that his prayers for help have been heard. He resolves to praise the Lord in the midst of his fellow worshipers and to invite them to do likewise. Verse 24 clearly states the reason: "For he hath not despised ... the affliction of the afflicted; neither hath he hid his face from him; but when he cried unto him, he heard."

The salty man of the Psalms did not easily come to terms with the doubts that stemmed from God's apparent forsaking of him. His inability to communicate with God had disturbed him even more than his taunting enemies. Obviously, however, he never completely gave up hope that God would intervene. God answered the prayers of the righteous man, and the man, in turn, publicly praised and thanked God. Once again, faith had overcome doubt.

People of our day (even Christians) often fall short on faith and long on doubt when prolonged trouble comes. They assume that unless God gives instant relief, he has forsaken them. Even when they do receive relief, they forget to thank and praise God who answered their cry for help.

For people like these, and for all of us, the psalmist has a message in Psalm 22. (1) Reaching the limits of your own strength does not mean that you have also reached the limits of God's strength. God can do for you what you cannot do for yourself. (2) No matter how severe your distress may be, be patient in waiting for the Lord. Do not let your inner doubts rise above your faith. When you do recognize God's presence (and you will!), respond with thanksgiving and praise. The spiritually salty person of every generation will cope with transient doubts and/or unresolved questions of faith by remaining open to God's leading and being responsive to his will.

Psalm 13

¹How long wilt thou forget me, O Lord? for ever? how long wilt thou hide thy face from me?

²How long shall I take counsel in my soul, having sorrow in my heart daily? how long shall mine enemy be exalted over me?

³Consider and hear me, O Lord my God: lighten mine eyes, lest I sleep the sleep of death;

⁴Lest mine enemy say, I have prevailed against him; and those that trouble me rejoice when I am moved.

⁵But I have trusted in thy mercy; my heart shall rejoice in thy salvation.

⁶I will sing unto the Lord, because he hath dealt bountifully with me.

The first psalm that we studied in this chapter (Ps. 77) showed how the righteous man's recognition of God's "quiet work" helped him to cope with doubts about God's answering his prayer. Psalm 13 approaches the problem of doubt from a slightly different perspective. In this psalm the worshiper showed his saltness by looking to the future with eyes of faith instead of surrendering to his fears and doubts. Both psalms contain frank confessions of a struggle with doubt, but equally frank conclusions that God can be completely trusted.

In spite of its brevity, Psalm 13 carries an important message for all who have grown weary of waiting for God to grant relief. In a nutshell, the message of Psalm 13 is: No matter how dark the shadows of life seem, light exists beyond them. God will not leave his people in the deep darkness forever.

The psalmist gets to the point immediately in this psalm. He wastes no time narrating the background or supplying the details. Nevertheless, worshipers of every generation can empathize with his agony as he cries, "How long wilt thou forget me, O Lord? for ever? how long wilt thou hide thy face from me?" (v. 1)

Verse 2 continues to narrate the plight of the righteous man. The worshiper neither hides nor ignores his problem. Candidly and with great feeling, he airs his grievances and confesses his impatience. He has grown weary of bearing pain and sorrow daily, but the problem does not end there. He is also galled because his enemies have ridiculed him because of his plight.

The expressions of impatience in verses 1-2 change to an earnest prayer in verses 3-4. The righteous man pleads with God to consider and answer his appeals for help. More specifically, he says: "Lighten mine eyes, lest I sleep the sleep of death" (v. 3).

The meaning of the words of verse 3 is not absolutely clear. The worshiper may be referring to the dullness of the eyes of an ill person, a dullness that disappears with the return of good health. On the other hand, it may simply be a reference to the effect of mental anguish on the eyes (for example, heaviness, dullness, redness). In that case the worshiper may mean, in the last clause of verse 3, that he fears he will remain sorrowful to his dying days. A third interpretation of the verse is that the worshiper is speaking figuratively about the eyes of faith. He recognizes that he must work through a period of doubt. He seeks God's spiritual enlightenment so that he can feel renewed and strengthened in faith.

The prayer continues in verse 4. How will the enemies of the righteous man react if God does not restore him? They will say, "I have prevailed against him" and will rejoice at his shaken faith. The thought expressed here does not reflect a desire to see the enemy destroyed, but rather to prove to the enemy that righteousness will be rewarded. The implication seems to be that restoration of the worshiper will both defend God's claim of power and preserve a faithful worshiper.

Verses 5-6 form a climax in the psalm. In reading these verses we might automatically assume that time had elapsed between the writing of the first four and last two verses. This was not necessarily the case, however. In ancient days men of faith often spoke of the future as though it had already come to pass. We might compare them to people who can visualize what the sunrise will look like, even though they are currently in the darkness of night.

The righteous man of Psalm 13 looked beyond his present plight and recognized that God had not forsaken him after all. Only through the eyes of faith could he anticipate the time when he would be delivered from the dark days he was experiencing. Although he had struggled with doubt and fear, he had not succumbed to it. In the last analysis he discovered that his faith was stronger than his doubts.

The righteous man's salt had not lost its savor in spite of what had transpired. In confident trust he could still say, "But I have trusted in thy mercy; my heart shall rejoice in thy salvation. I will sing unto the Lord, because he hath dealt bountifully with me" (vv. 5-6).

John had been able to grasp and respond to the simple message of the gospel in spite of his handicaps. He loved to attend church, even though he did not always understand everything that he heard. One night at prayer meeting he asked the pastor, "Preacher, when I get to heaven, will I still have to live in this same crippled body?" An expression of relief came over his face when the pastor assured him that he would have a new body after his earthly life. John could cope with the questions and doubts brought about by his present condition if he knew that God would remedy his situation in the future.

At times the only way to cope with doubt is to accept our present existence, dark though it may be, and look to the future with confident hope. Christ's promise to his followers of eternal life provides us with a valid reason to be optimistic. With the hope of a better future existence, we can more easily tolerate the uncertainty of the present.

Chapter 5
The Righteous Man
Interprets Nature

Psalm 19

[1]The heavens declare the glory of God; and the firmament sheweth his handiwork.

[2]Day unto day uttereth speech, and night unto night sheweth knowledge.

[3]There is no speech nor language, where their voice is not heard.

[4]Their line is gone out through all the earth, and their words to the end of the world. In them hath he set a tabernacle for the sun,

[5]Which is as a bridegroom coming out of his chamber, and rejoiceth as a strong man to run a race.

[6]His going forth is from the end of the heaven, and his circuit unto the ends of it: and there is nothing hid from the heat thereof.

People of ancient times viewed the forces of nature with awe. Pagans attached not only many superstitious legends, but also many deities, to the various object and forces in nature. The heavenly bodies, the earth, the sea, the windstorm, and other manifestations of nature, all had their own gods. Anything that pagans could not understand was relegated to the mystic realm. Even the ancient Israelites had notions about nature that would sound strange to us.

The more perceptive worshipers of Yahweh (the Lord) viewed nature from a different perspective, however. For example, the psalmist interpreted all of nature, including the skies, as a testimony to God's existence and character. The saltness of this righteous man lay in the perspective from which he viewed nature in its varied forms. Through the psalms he composed, the psalmist helped to preserve Israel's memory of the Creator of the universe.

The three psalms selected to illustrate how the righteous man interpreted nature are Psalms 19, 29, and 8. Psalm 19 focuses on heaven and earth as a general testimony to God's creativity. Psalm 29 emphasizes God's power as revealed in nature. Psalm 8 interprets nature as evidence of God's glory.

We shall begin this section with a study of Psalm 19:1-6. Actually, Psalm 19 consists of two separate hymns. One deals with nature, the other with the law. For this reason, we will confine the study of Psalm 19 to the first six verses.

Just before composing this hymn, the psalmist had very likely been gazing into the skies, marveling at God's creation. As he looked upward, he had the sensation of seeing a vast array of witnesses, proclaiming God as Creator. The testimony of the skies was not a "once and for all" declaration. It conveyed a continuous happening ("are telling," v. 1, RSV). Constantly the heavens kept revealing the presence and majesty of God. Like a basic primer in school, the heavens expressed its message simply and clearly enough for even a slow learner to grasp its meaning. The vault of heaven ("firmament"), extending from one end of the earth to the other, illustrated God's creative genius.

In verse 2 the righteous man interprets day and night as unbroken recordings of God's marvelous works. Each of these divisions of time have their own distinctive revelation to give, yet their messages focus on the same testimony. The point of verse 2 is that day and night present a continuous witness of God's greatness.

The righteous man observes a paradox. Technically, the voice of heavens is not audible; it does not even have an articulate language to use as a tool for speech (v. 3). It has only a silent eloquence. Nevertheless, every person in every part of the world has the potential ability to understand nature's revelation of God. One view of the heavens is worth a thousand words!

The righteous man sees the testimony of the heavens as covering a vast expanse ("through all the earth," v. 4). He finds no geographical limit to its witness. Figuratively, the "line" spoken of in verse 4 is a measuring line, stretched out across the sky to indicate God's possession of the whole universe. Because of its prominence, the sun becomes the chief witness to God's greatness. The Lord has made a dwelling place ("tabernacle") in the heavens for the sun (v. 4).

The figure of the sun continues in verse 5. First, the righteous man describes the sun as a bridegroom—young, splendid, and vigorous. He parallels the description of the sun as a bridegroom with that of a strong man, fully prepared, and poised to run the race. Both figures convey the message that the sun has mighty power and can warm and light the whole earth. Again, however, the reader must remember that in making these comments the psalmist was not worshiping the sun, but rather the God who made the sun.

In summary, the righteous man showed his saltness in Psalm 19 by the way he interpreted nature. He did not view the skies as merely a domain to conquer or a beauty to behold or an object to worship. He interpreted the heavens as a silent, but effective witness of the greatness of the Lord whom he worshiped.

In the days of early Christianity an apostle of Christ picked up the psalmist's theme. The apostle viewed nature as a testimony to God's existence and greatness even for pagans who knew nothing about the living God (Acts 14:17). If nature's revelation of God served as a witness to pagans, surely it also continues to declare the glory and handiwork of God to Christians of our day.

Nevertheless, persons of today are faced with an interesting challenge relating to Psalm 19. In an era when the skies are filling with man-made pollution and sophisticated aircraft, Christians must look intently to see the message of the heavens. The salty Christian, however, will look beyond the ground and sky clutter created by man and see the marvels created by God. Like the psalmist, he will see, hear, and join in the refrain, as "the heavens declare the glory of God" (v. 1).

Psalm 29

¹Give unto the Lord, O ye mighty, give unto the Lord glory and strength.

. . . .

³The voice of the Lord is upon the waters: the God of glory thundereth: the Lord is upon many waters.

⁴The voice of the Lord is powerful; the voice of the Lord is full of majesty.

⁵The voice of the Lord breaketh the cedars; yea, the Lord breaketh the cedars of Lebanon.

. . . .

⁷The voice of the Lord divideth the flames of fire.

⁸The voice of the Lord shaketh the wilderness of Kadesh; the Lord shaketh the wilderness of Kadesh.

. . . .

¹⁰The Lord sitteth upon the flood; yea, the Lord sitteth King for ever.

¹¹The Lord will give strength unto his people; the Lord will bless his people with peace.

The power of God, as revealed in nature, created awe in the hearts of ancient people. Israel, especially, interpreted the great forces of nature from a religious viewpoint. For example, Habakkuk 3:10 pictures the mountains as trembling when they saw God. Psalm 8 depicts God as creator of nature. Psalm 29 ascribes to the Lord the status of "God of the storm." Each activity of nature had religious significance in the eyes of Israel. Even the presence of the various forms of nature testified to God's existence and power.

As shown in Psalm 29, however, the righteous man of the Psalter went beyond the view that nature had religious significance. Even pagans believed that storms manifested the anger of the gods. The righteous man reveals his salt in his response to the threat presented by a storm. He interprets the storm not as a threat to Israel's safety but rather as an evidence of God's power to protect. Verse 11 reveals that the righteous man recognizes that the God who has power to create the storms also has power to bless and strengthen his people. The worshiper's reminder has a calming influence on the covenant community.

Presumably the Israelites sang Psalm 29 at a festival, such as the Feast of Tabernacles. Its origin dates back to an early period of Israel's history.

The righteous man begins his poetic testimony of faith with a call to worship. He summons all the spiritual beings of heaven to praise and worship God: "Ascribe to the Lord, O heavenly beings ... glory and strength. Ascribe to the Lord the glory of his name; worship the Lord in holy array" (vv. 1-2, RSV).

The worshiper bases his current call to praise God on a mighty thunderstorm he sees brewing in the heavens. Verses 3-9 contain an account of the storm. The point of Psalm 29, however, is not to describe the terror of the storm but to give the righteous man's interpretation of the storm's religious significance.

Storms have been a source of fear among people through the ages. Are not the loud thunder and the threatening skies good reason to be frightened and to feel vulnerable and unprotected? Not so, says the righteous man of the Psalter. The roaring and rumbling that the Israelites hear should bring reassurance, not terror. The thunder is the voice of the Lord, manifesting his power and majesty so that his worshipers will see the greatness of their God (vv. 3-4). The righteous man becomes so awed by this evidence of God's power that he can think of nothing else.

He continues to marvel at the God of storms as he watches trees fall as a result of the lightning. (Ancient people, however, attributed destruction to thunder instead of to lightning, probably because of the impressive sound of thunder.) The tremendous cedar trees of Lebanon toppled in the wake of the storm (v. 5), yet even this fearsome sight did not distract the worshiper's train of thought. He heard in the crackling timber the powerful voice of God. Using poetic imagery, he speaks in verse 6 of how God causes the mountains of Lebanon to skip like a calf and Mount Hermon ("Sirion") like a young ox.

In verses 7-8 the righteous man continues his description of how God manifests himself in a storm. First, he speaks of God's revelation in the lightning ("flames of fire"). Ancient people believed that lightning issued from the mouth of God. The expression "the *voice* of the Lord divideth the flames of fire" probably refers to the idea that the voice comes through the mouth. The lightning followed the path of God's voice across the heavens. Furthermore, the righteous man adds: "The voice of the Lord shaketh the wilderness" (v. 8). The wilderness of Kadesh, usually known for its stillness, was visibly shaken by the storm.

Verse 10 heralds the end of the storm. "The Lord sits enthroned over the flood" (RSV). The righteous man concludes by repeating a theme that runs quietly throughout the account. That theme is the interpretation of storms as a positive manifestation of God's power rather than a negative one. A God who can manifest his strength in a storm can also protect his people and bless them with peace (v. 11).

A few years ago a destructive tornado hit the city of Louisville, Kentucky. People watched in terror as strong houses collapsed, trees uprooted, and cars were tossed into the air like flimsy toys. Some people interpreted the tornado as a natural disaster; others saw it as an act of God's judgment; still others felt too stunned to analyze it at all.

In retrospect, however, several Christians confessed that

the tornado caused them to see things in a new light. Material possessions could not compete in importance with human lives; helping one another became a necessity not an option; disaster provided an opportunity for Christian witness through community service. In this regard, some persons felt that the Lord "spoke" to them through the storm—not quite in the same way as the psalmist expressed it in Psalm 29, but clearly anyhow.

The God whose power extends over the storms of nature can also give strength to his people. Only when by faith we reach that conclusion, however, can we control our fear of storms. The righteous man of Psalm 29 learned to concentrate more on the power of God manifested in the storm than in personal fear because of the threats of the storm. That is a lesson some of us need to learn in order to become saltier Christians today.

Psalm 8

¹O Lord our Lord, how excellent is thy name in all the earth! who hast set thy glory above the heavens.

²Out of the mouth of babes and sucklings hast thou ordained strength because of thine enemies, that thou mightest still the enemy and the avenger.

³When I consider thy heavens, the work of thy fingers, the moon and the stars, which thou hast ordained;

⁴What is man, that thou art mindful of

him? and the son of man, that thou visitest him?

⁵For thou hast made him a little lower than the angels, and hast crowned him with glory and honour.

⁶Thou madest him to have dominion over the works of thy hands; thou hast put all things under his feet:

⁷All sheep and oxen, yea, and the beasts of the field;

⁸The fowl of the air, and the fish of the sea, and whatsoever passeth through the paths of the seas.

⁹O Lord our Lord, how excellent is thy name in all the earth!

Psalm 8 is one of the most beautiful and beloved psalms in the Psalter. This hymn of praise to God has two themes. One of the themes is man's status in God's universe—a very real concern for people of every generation. However, Psalm 8 also focuses on another important theme: the role of nature in witnessing to God's glory. This latter theme places the psalm appropriately in this chapter.

We cannot be certain about the occasion for the writing of this psalm. The descriptions of nature found in the psalm suggest the possibility that David wrote it during his time as a shepherd in the fields. Certainly the quietness of the open pasture would be conducive to meditations on the marvels of nature. Regardless of the exact circumstance of the writing, though, the meaning of the psalm is clear. The psalmist interprets nature not as merely a show-window for the sake of its own glory, but rather as a testimony of the glory of the Creator.

Psalm 8 is a psalm for all times. Israel sang it at special festivals in Old Testament times. Job 7:17 makes a brief reference to it. The New Testament contains quotations from it, for example in Hebrews 2:6-8 and 1 Corinthians 15:27. People of our day frequently quote Psalm 8.

Appropriately, the righteous man of the Psalms begins his meditations with words of praise for the Creator (v. 1). As he gazes into the heavens, he seems to do it with new perception. He envisions the heavens as a giant banner that testifies about God's glory, or a mighty choir singing praises to the Lord. He reflects that the whole earth recognizes the majesty of God's name and creativity. All that the nations must do to recognize it is to heed the testimony of the heavens.

The righteous man examines the matter further. He marvels as he realizes that even young children perceive the wonder of creation; in fact, children sometimes perceive what more sophisticated adults fail to recognize. One of the marvels about God is his ability to reveal great truths to small people, truths so sublime that they silence the more worldly-wise scoffer (v. 2). Nature, according to the interpretation of this ancient worshiper, did not reserve its testimony of God's glory only for the high and mighty members of the community. Nature did it for *all* persons who inhabited the earth to see.

As the righteous man considers God's work of creation (the heavens containing the moon and stars), he puzzles over a profound question. What significance does man have in all this vast universe? Why should God even notice man, much less continuously care for him? (v. 4).

The amazement of the worshiper increases even more as he recalls how much God did to elevate man in the universe. God made man only a little lower than the "angels" (v. 5, KJV) or "God" (RSV). The statement in Genesis

1:26-28 relating to God's creation of man seems to support the RSV translation here. The worshiper further observes that God crowned man with glory and honor. He uses the figure of God's making men into kings, as it were. This figure is especially interesting in view of the fact that in ancient times, people considered human kings to be earthly representatives of the heavenly King.

The righteous man's thoughts linger on the meaning of the honor that God bestowed on man. All creatures on earth are subject to man. He has dominion over the sheep, oxen, beasts, fowls of the air, fish of the sea, and other inhabitants of the sea (v. 8). This by no means exhausts the list of the creatures over which man has dominion. It merely serves as an illustrative list.

The last verse of Psalm 8 provides us with a plain clue as to how the righteous man views not only the marvels of nature but also the honored status of man. The Lord alone merits credit for all that has been done. Every part of creation signifies the glory of God. The heavens above, beautiful though they are, are not there for self-glorification. They function as a witness to the greatness of God. Man did not receive a place of honor and dominion in order that he could have cause to boast. He received this gift through the gracious power of God. Nature and man have a common purpose: to become testimonies of God's glory. The self-interpretation of the righteous man of the Psalter is a foreshadow of the salty apostle of Christ who said, "He that glorieth, let him glory in the Lord" (1 Cor. 1:31).

In a spirit of wonder and reverence, the righteous man concludes his meditation with the words with which he began it: "O Lord our Lord, how excellent is thy name in all the earth!" (v. 9).

On display in a gift shop is a ceramic figure of an ape. The large ape holds in his hand a small human skull. The puzzled expression on the ape's face as he studies the skull seems to communicate the question: What is so great about man?

Many modern people have become so impressed with their own accomplishments that they have lost their perspective. True, compared to the lower animals, people of today may seem great. Compared to God, however, we are nothing.

Salty worshipers of our day interpret both nature and the status of mankind in proper perspective. Nature is marvelous because God made it that way. It testifies to God's glory. Mankind has a status of dignity and dominion because God graciously put him there. Thus, man, too, serves as a witness to God's glory. God, not man, reigns in the universe. With the psalmist let us join in this refrain of praise to God: "How majestic is thy name in all the earth!" (v. 9, RSV).

Chapter 6
The Righteous Man
Responds to Success

Psalm 66

¹Make a joyful noise unto God, all ye lands:

²Sing forth the honour of his name: make his praise glorious.

³Say unto God, How terrible art thou in thy works! through the greatness of thy power shall thine enemies submit themselves unto thee.

⁴All the earth shall worship thee, and shall sing unto thee; they shall sing to thy name. Selah.

. . . .

¹⁰For thou, O God, hast proved us: thou hast tried us, as silver is tried.

¹¹Thou broughtest us into the net; thou laidst affliction upon our loins.

¹²Thou hast caused men to ride over our heads; we went through fire and through water: but thou broughtest us out into a wealthy place.

¹³I will go into thy house with burnt offerings: I will pay thee my vows.

. . . .

[20]Blessed be God, which hath not turned away my prayer, nor his mercy from me.

Very few rational people would argue the need to learn to cope with *hard* times when they come. In order to survive, we must learn to cope with less than ideal situations. How many persons, however, recognize a like need to cope effectively with success when it comes?

Learning to handle success responsibly can be a challenging process for a conscientious worshiper. By its very nature, success exposes a person to new temptations and even a new life-style. Jesus recognized this problem during his earthly ministry and tried to teach his disciples some important lessons about the proper attitude toward, and response to, worldly success. Some of Jesus' teachings were quite revolutionary, even in the religious world of his day. Statements such as those found in Matthew 5:16 and John 15:8 have given Christians throughout the centuries new insights into the way they should handle success.

Part of the saltness of believers, whether in the Christian era or in Old Testament days, has been in the example set for handling success. People of the psalmist's day still measured success largely in terms of military victory or material prosperity. This view conflicts with Jesus' later interpretation of success. Nevertheless, in proportion to the light he had, the righteous man of the Psalter exerted his saltness in the way he viewed the origin of and proper response to success.

Psalms 66, 67, and 124 illustrate the saltness of the worshiper in his response to success. The first of the three psalms (Ps. 66) illustrates the proper response on three levels: international, national, and personal. Israel very likely applied this psalm later to the celebration of Passover, but its original use related to a specific happening, such as military victory. One of the interesting features of Psalm 66 is the way the thought pattern moves from corporate to individual causes for thanksgiving to God for victory and prosperity.

As Psalm 66 opens, the righteous man has evidently approached the altar to present his thanksgiving offering. The sacrificial act causes him to reflect on the universal need to recognize God's role in the prosperity of the whole world. He summons all nations to acknowledge how much they owe God for his mercy toward them (vv. 1-4).

In verses 5-7 the righteous man renews his open invitation to join in worship and thanksgiving. He assumes that all nations, even ones hostile to Israel, cannot ignore the power of God in history. He recalls to their minds two especially successful ventures in the history of Israel. They are Israel's deliverance from the clutches of Egypt when the Red Sea divided (Ex. 14:21) and the stopping of the Jordan River which enabled the people of God to cross (Josh. 3:11-17). Notice how carefully he places the credit for these successes where they should be—in the power and grace of God. The worshiper reminds his listeners that this same God keeps his eyes on every nation. Thus, all rulers and nations should beware of exalting themselves above the Lord (v. 7).

The righteous man moves from a plea for universal praise of God to one on a national level in verses 8-12. He contends that the covenant community had special reason to offer thanks to God for giving her prosperity and success after an experience of affliction (v. 12). The righteous man recalls times in his nation's history when the outlook did not appear this hopeful. He admits that his nation's achieve-

ment of success did not come easy; in fact, at times his
people did well just to survive (v. 9). The words "caused
men to ride over our heads" (v. 12) refers to the Egyptian
and Assyrian practice of driving their carts over the bodies
of conquered enemies. The righteous man views the testing,
afflictions, and defeats as a preparation for the better times.
Therefore, he reasons that the nation has cause to thank
God not only for deliverance into victory and prosperity, but
also for the apparent disasters.

The thoughts of the worshiper presenting his offering
now turn toward his individual situation (vv. 13-20). Obviously, this righteous man feels that God has blessed him as
a person in an abundant fashion. He remembers that just as
his whole nation had experienced trouble in the past, so had
he personally faced trouble. In his time of distress the righteous man had promised that if God would deliver him, he
would not forget God's grace (vv. 14-15). The righteous
man intends to keep his word. For him, this would be no
deathbed promise to God, then forgetfulness in good
health. The generous sacrifice he makes is proof of his gratitude and his recognition of the source of his present success. The righteous man set a public example of saltness for
his own generation. As verses 18-20 point out, however,
God would not have heeded these prayers for success if
they had come from an unrighteous man. Because of his
faith, the worshiper had received the favor and blessing of
God who made his success possible.

As pointed out earlier, Jesus redefined the meaning of
success during his earthly ministry. Nevertheless, he re-
tained the same emphasis as the psalmist: The proper response to success is gratitude to God. Haughtiness and
vanity are unworthy traits for a Christian to cultivate.

We have a modern-day saying, "It is hard to be humble
when you are so great!" The saying is of the tongue-in-

cheek variety, but it does reflect the attitude of many modern-day successes. Christ said, "He that is greatest among you shall be your servant" (Matt. 23:11). When viewed from this perspective, success becomes less self-exalting.

Through careful investments and a lifetime of frugal spending, a Christian couple accumulated a considerable savings account. From outward appearances, the couple gave no indication of wealth. They had a modest home and no extravagant possessions. The news came as a shock, therefore, when they announced privately that they planned to give eventually a substantial amount of money for the education of ministerial students.

The fact that the couple had accumulated that much money signified success in the eyes of the world. Typically for the couple, however, the man and his wife viewed their success only as an opportunity to contribute to the work of God's kingdom on earth. They really did not want their name to be disclosed. They simply loved the Lord and appreciated his goodness to them. The financial outlay served as one way that they could show their gratitude.

This true story exemplifies saltness in the face of success. Like the psalmist, the couple recognized the source of their blessing and wanted to respond in an appropriate way.

Psalm 67

[1]God be merciful unto us, and bless us; and cause his face to shine upon us; Selah. [2]That thy way may be known upon earth, thy saving health among all nations.

³Let the people praise thee, O God; let all the people praise thee.

⁴O let the nations be glad and sing for joy: for thou shalt judge the people righteously, and govern the nations upon earth. Selah.

⁵Let the people praise thee, O God; let all the people praise thee.

⁶Then shall the earth yield her increase; and God, even our own God, shall bless us.

⁷God shall bless us; and all the ends of the earth shall fear him.

As indicated in the study of the preceding psalm, ancient nations usually measured success by worldly values, such as material or military success. Psalm 67 rises somewhat above the norm in that respect. Although Psalm 67 was used as a communal thanksgiving hymn for harvest, it crossed national boundaries and went beyond material values. This hymn encompassed not only Israel, but all the nations of the earth. Furthermore, success included, but also transcended worldly prosperity. It rose to a higher level, that of the spiritual prosperity of God's purpose for all mankind.

Psalm 67 opens with a portion of a blessing familiar to Jews and Christians alike. In fact, many churches of today use it as a part of their worship service. Actually, verse 1 is a partial quotation of the ancient blessing given by Aaron: "The Lord bless thee, and keep thee: The Lord make his face shine upon thee, and be gracious unto thee: The Lord lift up his countenance upon thee, and give thee peace" (Num. 6:24-26).

The righteous man of Psalm 67 was speaking in behalf of his fellow worshipers as they gathered to thank God for the harvest. His thoughts would naturally focus on the success of the agricultural season. Without God's gracious blessing, the abundant harvest would be impossible. The sun, rain, and fertility of the soil that made possible a good crop came as a gift of God. By recognizing the source of harvest success, the worshiper averted the danger described in Deuteronomy 6:11-12: "When thou shalt have eaten and be full . . . beware lest thou forget the Lord."

Verse 2 pictures the thoughts of the righteous man as moving beyond the covenant community and his immediate cause for giving thanks. He envisions a wider scope and loftier type of success. With spiritual perception beyond most Israelites of his day, he directs his thoughts toward other nations and their place in God's plan. If other nations see how much God has done for Israel, they will know that he can also deliver them. The righteous man summons all the nations to acknowledge God's power and praise his name (v. 3).

The evangelistic flavor of verse 3 continues throughout the remainder of the psalm. The worshiper anticipates the time when the other nations of the world shall join Israel in hymns of gladness and joy. The world will see that the God of Israel is in reality the God of the universe. The Lord governs and leads all the nations of earth in the eventual fulfillment of his purpose. For this reason, not only Israel but *all* nations should join together in a hymn of praise to God (vv. 4-5). The focus in verses 3-5 rested on the desire for God's name to be exalted throughout the world—success from a spiritual standpoint. This was an enlightened concept at a time when Israel frequently viewed other nations as her enemies and cherished her own special favor in God's sight.

The thoughts of the righteous man return to the purpose for which he had come to worship, that of giving thanks for the success of the harvest. "The earth has yielded its increase; God, our God, has blessed us" (v. 6, RSV). The worshiper gives credit for the abundant harvest to the one to whom it belonged, the gracious provider of all life's blessings.

Psalm 67 concludes on an optimistic note. The success of which the righteous man speaks in verse 7 has both material and spiritual elements and applies on both a national and international level. The abundance of the harvest can have a redemptive effect on those who observe it. Other nations will hold in awe the Lord who made possible this successful harvest.

The righteous man of Psalm 67 showed his saltness in two respects: (1) by leading his fellow worshipers to respond to the harvest blessing with thanksgiving; (2) by seeing in the harvest a means of glorifying God in the sight of other nations. His concept of success rose above the selfish, materialistic level to a spiritual level. He hoped that all nations would recognize what God had done for Israel and praise God because of it.

Salty worshipers of today do not automatically "believe their own press reports"; that is, they do not take seriously the exaggerated claims about their accomplishments. They recognize that a little talent can go a long way when supplemented by God's reinforcing strength.

Furthermore, a salty worshiper knows that the greatest success does not come in the material realm but in the spiritual one. He recalls Jesus' statement, "For what is a man profited, if he shall gain the whole world, and lose his own soul?" (Matt. 16:26). He does not fall into the same trap as the worldly wise man who thinks that material success alone will buy happiness and lasting peace.

The salty worshiper of our day remembers to thank God for whatever his success is, then asks himself: Now, how can I bring honor to God through this success?

Psalm 124

¹If it had not been the Lord who was on our side, now may Israel say;
²If it had not been the Lord who was on our side, when men rose up against us:
³Then they had swallowed us up quick, when their wrath was kindled against us:
⁴Then the waters had overwhelmed us, the stream had gone over our soul:
⁵Then the proud waters had gone over our soul.
⁶Blessed be the Lord, who hath not given us as a prey to their teeth.
⁷Our soul is escaped as a bird out of the snare of the fowlers: the snare is broken, and we are escaped.
⁸Our help is in the name of the Lord, who made heaven and earth.

Success on the military level was a high cause of thanksgiving for Israel. Psalm 124 serves as an example of how the righteous man of the Psalter responded to military success and how he led his fellow worshipers to do likewise. The writer does not identify whether the psalm refers to the out-come of a specific battle or a composite of many battles. However, no doubt can remain in the reader's mind as to the purpose of the psalm: to offer thanks to God for military deliverance from extreme danger.

Israél adopted Psalm 124 for congregational use at times of communal thanksgiving. Israel's history shows that God often delivered his people from the kind of battle described in this psalm. Therefore, the words of the psalm likely brought back many memories, especially to the elders of Israel.

Psalm 124 opens with almost startling abruptness. Evidently the righteous man had been mulling over in his mind the danger to which he and his nation had been exposed. He suddenly begins to speak aloud his thoughts. Israel could have easily been swallowed up by her enemy if it had not been for the fact that the Lord was on Israel's side! (vv. 1-3).

The figure "swallowed us up alive" (v. 3, RSV) is a graphic one. Jeremiah used it to describe Babylon's devouring of Jerusalem (Jer. 51:34). It conveys the idea of a sea monster swallowing his prey. The psalmist uses the figure in Psalm 124 to express his terror about how close the enemy had come to devouring Israel during the military battle.

The real point of the righteous man's statement in verses 1-3, however, is that the Lord was on Israel's side. The concept of the Lord as "God of battles" goes back to Exodus 14:14. There Moses told his fearful people, "The Lord shall fight for you, and ye shall hold your peace." The righteous man felt convinced that once again the Lord had fought for Israel. Israel had been able to escape being swallowed up by the enemy *only* because of the Lord's help. The worshiper knew that the story could have ended very differently if the Lord had not empowered Israel. The current incident provided the righteous man and his fellow Israelites with a fresh look at the importance of receiving God's help.

The imagery of the sea monster swallowing up his prey leads the righteous man to think of a second metaphor to describe the situation. This time the worshiper pictures his enemies as a torrential flood, ready to sweep away its victims. In Isaiah 8:7-8, the prophet used the same imagery to describe a military situation in which Assyria was about to inundate Judah. In Psalm 124 the psalmist used the metaphor of the enemy as a raging flood in a similar fashion. His point was that without God's help, Israel would have met destruction.

In verses 6-7 the righteous man adds two more figures of speech to depict Israel's former plight. First, he speaks of Israel's deliverance from the teeth of wild beasts. The meaning is like that of Psalm 7:2, where he describes the enemy as a lion, waiting to tear up the righteous man. Second, he compares Israel's narrow escape with that of a bird caught in a net but freed when the snare broke. Israel, like a bird, escaped what could have been a disaster. The nation had almost been trapped!

The righteous man recognized that Israel did not receive deliverance because of the skill of her warriors but rather because of the help provided by the Lord. God had made possible Israel's successful escape (v. 8).

The righteous man of the Psalter responded to military success by acknowledging God as the source of his help. The beginning words of his testimony illustrate the saltness which permeates the whole psalm: "If it had not been the Lord who was on our side, when men rose up against us: Then they had swallowed us up quick" (vv. 2-3).

Psalm 124 dealt with victory in a military crisis, but many of the battles of life are not military ones. Modern worshipers must war against such enemies as temptation, frustration, poverty, disease, loneliness, and failure. Without the faith to know that the Lord is on our side, we could be swallowed up by such enemies. Only with God's help can we learn to cope with these foes that create crises in our lives.

A middle-aged Christian felt devastated when the doctor told him that he was terminally ill. This became a crisis of great magnitude for the Christian. He brooded over all his unfinished business and unfulfilled goals, struggling in his efforts to come to terms with what had happened. Inwardly he even began to blame God for his plight. In his anguish, he saw God as his enemy.

Finally, however, after he had worked through some of his hostility, he picked up the Bible that he had once cherished so much. As he thumbed through the New Testament, he felt a strange compulsion to stop at 1 Corinthians 15:54-57. The passage read: "Death is swallowed up in victory. O death, where is thy sting? O grave, where is thy victory? . . . thanks be to God, which giveth us the victory through our Lord Jesus Christ."

Suddenly the Christian realized that the Lord was still on his side after all. Death might swallow up the man's body, but God would bring him the ultimate victory of resurrection. The saltness of the Christian again became manifest when he could pray: "Thank you, Lord, for rescuing me from the defeat of death and bringing me to the victory of eternal life. Truly you are my Redeemer and Deliverer."

Chapter 7
The Righteous Man
Contends with Failure

Psalm 32

[1]Blessed is he whose transgression is forgiven, whose sin is covered.

[2]Blessed is the man unto whom the Lord imputeth not iniquity, and in whose spirit there is no guile.

[3]When I kept silence, my bones waxed old through my roaring all the day long.

[4]For day and night thy hand was heavy upon me: my moisture is turned into the drought of summer. Selah.

[5]I acknowledged my sin unto thee, and mine iniquity have I not hid. I said, I will confess my transgressions unto the Lord; and thou forgavest the iniquity of my sin. Selah.

. . . .

[9]Be ye not as the horse, or as the mule, which have no understanding: whose mouth must be held in with bit and bridle, lest they come near unto thee.

[10]Many sorrows shall be to the wicked: but he that trusteth in the Lord, mercy shall compass him about.

Failure can take many shapes, depending on one's perspective. Some paradoxes from the New Testament illustrate the role of perspective in deciding what constitutes failure. To find is to lose (Matt. 10:39), to die is gain (Phil. 1:21), and persecution is cause for rejoicing (Matt. 5:11-12). For unbelievers, of course, a completely different set of standards of failure and success exists.

The righteous man of the Psalter, steeped in the traditions of his own culture, recognized few "gray" areas in determining what constitutes failure. For example, military defeat spelled disgrace; poverty came with loss of divine favor; affliction was punishment; persecution meant disaster. However, at least one important element of his theology agreed with that held by Christ: sin is a failure of the worst kind. The only remedy for it is repentance, confession, and forgiveness. Other signs of failure with which the righteous man had to contend will be pointed out in the discussions of Psalms 38 and 79. Psalm 32 will serve as a basis for the initial discussion, since it so closely parallels the high quality of saltness that Christ expected of his disciples in dealing with this problem.

Many scholars believe that David composed Psalm 32 after his sin with Bathsheba and his murder of her husband (2 Sam. 11). Clearly, Psalm 32 deals with an experience of great sin in the life of a member of the covenant community. It is a highly personal confession of how one man attempted to conceal his sin from God and was almost destroyed by his own folly before he acknowledged his error. He demonstrates his pre-Christian saltness in coping with the failure known as sin by his repentance, confession, and receipt of forgiveness. His sincere penitence and his attempt to warn others against disobedience toward God exemplified to the community how a righteous man should contend with failure.

Psalm 32 begins with the statement of a blessing arrived at only after a painful experience. Happy is the person who does not have to carry the burden of unforgiven sin (v. 1). From personal experience, the righteous man has learned the torture of having God's fellowship withdrawn from him. Conversely, he also knows the joy of being back in God's favor. The wording of the first two verses of this psalm suggests three general categories of unrighteousness: (1) transgression—rebellion against God; (2) sin—missing the mark, and (3) iniquity—moral distortion. The real point of verses 1-2, however, is not what kind of sin he committed, but the fact that the sinner no longer tries to deceive himself and God about his need of forgiveness (v. 2).

In retrospect the worshiper recalls the mental anguish and actual physical pain he endured before he confessed his guilt honestly and openly to God. He speaks of how he deteriorated physically during his ordeal. "His bones waxed old" (v. 3) refers to the fact that the framework of his body felt feeble and ached, like the bones of an old man. He lost his vitality as though he were dehydrated (v. 4). His guilty conscience, the instrument of God's wrath and eventual redemption, would not let up its torment. It pounded on him day and night.

Verse 5 is the key verse of the psalm. It reveals two facts about the man that parallel the requirement that Christ later made on those who would follow him. First, he met God's demand of total honesty by acknowledging his guilt. Second, he made his confession in a spirit of penitence. Like people of today, the ancient man needed to ask God's forgiveness for his wrongdoing. Verse 5 suggests an interesting paradox that brings to mind the ones found in the Gospels. The fallen "righteous man" of the Psalter had to bring his sin out in the open where it would be plainly *seen* before the sin could be *covered* so that it would not be seen! Regardless of the man's penitence, however, the grace of God, not the confession of the man, ultimately made forgiveness possible. If God had not laid his hand heavy on the man (v. 4), the man's conscience might not have been stirred to repentance. Furthermore, if God had not chosen to forgive and restore him to fellowship, all the penitence in the world would have gained him nothing (v. 5).

The psalmist devotes the remainder of the psalm to helping the rest of the covenant community profit from the mistake of the erring worshiper. He first advises them to stay close to the Lord at all times, never withholding honest confession of sin nor failing to ask forgiveness. By following that advice, they will not risk having to endure the mental anguish of not being able to reach out for God's help when they need it. The grace of God can preserve and deliver one from all kinds of trouble, but God's help must be sought in order to be found.

Experience can be a good teacher if godly people will let it. The forgiven man counsels his fellow worshipers not to behave like a horse or mule as he had (v. 9). Persons should not have to be bridled like lower animals to achieve obedience; they should submit willingly. The Revised Standard Version translates verse 9 in a manner understandable today: "Be not like a horse or mule,/without understanding,/which must be curbed with bit and bridle,/else it will not keep with you." In other words, do not make God force you to draw near to him and obey him.

In spite of the worshiper's slowness to acknowledge his sins, he does eventually conquer his inner battle and find peace and forgiveness. He can now say with conviction, "Many are the pangs of the wicked; but steadfast love surrounds him who trusts in the Lord" (v. 10, RSV). He concludes his testimony with a summons to the whole community of the righteous to rejoice in the grace of God for the blessedness of forgiven sin.

The saltness of the righteous man in contending with sin parallels that of first-century Christianity: "If we say that we have no sin, we deceive ourselves, and the truth is not in us. If we confess our sins, he is faithful and just to forgive us our sins, and to cleanse us from all unrighteousness" (1 John 1:8-9).

Last year a preacher announced as his sermon topic, "Whatever Happened to Repentance?" His point was well taken. Modern society focuses on *not* acknowledging guilt, rather than confessing it. We punish ourselves needlessly if we carry a burden of guilt *after* receiving forgiveness. Nevertheless, refusal to accept responsibility for one's conduct and to repent of the sin is even more self-defeating.

In a very real way, sin signifies failure. The only valid solution to this kind of failure is the one used by the psalmist: repent, and confess your sin to the Lord, asking his forgiveness. Like the psalmist, you will discover, "I acknowledged my sin unto thee ... and thou forgavest the iniquity of my sin" (Ps. 32:5).

Psalm 38

¹O Lord, rebuke me not in thy wrath: neither chasten me in thy hot displeasure.
²For thine arrows stick fast in me, and thy hand presseth me sore.
³There is no soundness in my flesh be-

cause of thine anger; neither is there any
rest in my bones because of my sin.

. . . .

⁶I am troubled; I am bowed down greatly;
I go mourning all the day long.
⁷For my loins are filled with a loathsome
disease: and there is no soundness in my
flesh.
⁸I am feeble and sore broken: I have
roared by reason of the disquietness of my
heart.

. . . .

¹¹My lovers and my friends stand aloof
from my sore; and my kinsmen stand afar
off.

. . . .

¹⁸For I will declare mine iniquity; I will
be sorry for my sin.

. . . .

²¹Forsake me not, O Lord: O my God, be
not far from me.
²²Make haste to help me, O Lord my salvation.

In the previous psalm we saw how the righteous man
contended with one form of failure—sin. Specifically, the sin
dealt with in Psalm 32 was adultery. We need to keep in
mind, however, that the Israelites thought that all failure
resulted from sin, either one of ignorance (Lev. 4:2) or a
deliberate one. Thus, the Israelites viewed sin both as a *type*
of failure and the *cause* of failure.

Psalm 38, therefore, assumes that the failure (in this instance, ill health) resulted from some kind of sin. Psalm 38 gives us no clue as to the kind of sin that the basically righteous man had presumably committed. In studying the psalm we will view it from the perspective of how an ancient worshiper contended with a health failure.

This psalm falls into the category known as penitential or lament psalms. The title of the psalm notes that the Israelites used the hymn when they presented memorial offerings. Today some churches use it in Ash Wednesday services.

The opening words of Psalm 38 immediately introduce us to the reason for the prayer of the righteous man. Convinced that his present ill health (both physical and mental) came as punishment for sin, the worshiper appeals to the Lord for mercy. He does not deny the possibility that he may have sinned, nor does he doubt God's justice in punishing him. He makes his petition purely on the basis of God's mercy.

"O Lord, rebuke me not in thy wrath . . . for thine arrows stick fast in me" (vv. 1-2), he says. The health failure with which the righteous man must contend has caused him great suffering. He does not deny guilt; likely, he learned from his youth up that sickness came as punishment for sin. Thus, the matter that perplexes him is not whether he deserves punishment, but why the punishment is so severe.

The "arrows" of which the righteous man speaks in verse 2 are God's judgment in the form of illness. He feels that God has pierced him with the arrows of ill health, coming down upon his whole being with a heavy hand. The implied question seems to be: How can a loving God be so unmerciful in his punishment of one of his own chosen people?

The righteous man finds that he has been assaulted by a two-headed arrow. One arrowhead (God's wrath) pierces him from the outside; the other arrowhead (his guilt-feelings) pierces him from the inside (v. 3). The suffering he must endure because of his sins has become too much for him.

In verse 6 the righteous man speaks of being troubled, bowed down, in mourning. He may be referring to the fact that his suffering body bends with pain. He also may mean that he is a penitent mourner, recognizing that his illness resulted from his sin. He has a loathsome disease. He experiences "burning" (v. 7, RSV, probably denoting fever and inflammation). Feeble and crushed because of what has happened to him, the man moans pitifully. Verse 9 indicates that he feels certain that God can hear his cries, even if he does not respond.

The righteous man thinks that everyone has deserted him. At the very time when he most needs the supportive love of his family and friends, he finds them standing aloof from him. As for his enemies, they take advantage of his plight by plotting all the more against him, knowing that he dare not open his mouth (vv. 11-14).

Verses 15-22 depict a man who knows that his only hope rests in the Lord. He cannot pull himself up by his own bootstraps, and he cannot depend on his family and friends to do it for him. At this time of failure in his life, he makes his appeal to the one source that can help him—God. In a spirit of humility, penitence, and faith, the ancient worshiper casts himself upon God's mercy.

The saltness of the righteous man in contending with failure was not a matter of self-reliance, but of God-reliance. It did not result from knowing the right people, but in knowing the Lord. Furthermore, his saltness was not in pleading innocence or in making excuses for whatever conduct may have brought on the punishment of ill health (v. 18).

The worshiper's health, family, and friends had all failed him. Nevertheless, he did not give up. Through the eyes of faith he could anticipate that God would eventually lift him above these failures; the question was simply a matter of "when?" The righteous man's concluding appeal in verse 22 reflects urgency, but it also reflects trust. He has faith to believe that God will help those who look to him for deliverance.

Psalm 38 cannot be taken "whole meal" as the Christian philosophy of dealing with health and handicap problems. Although sin *can* still contribute to health failure, it is certainly not the only possible cause. Jesus himself taught that God sometimes allows health or handicap problems to come to persons for a positive, rather than a negative, purpose (John 9:3). In addition to the purpose mentioned in the Gospel of John, you can probably think of other positive purposes that ill health or handicap have served at times.

Nevertheless, the psalmist does point to some relevant ways in which true worshipers of today can contend effectively with health failure. We can examine our lives to see if, indeed, we have brought it on ourselves through misconduct; and if we have, we can repent and ask God's forgiveness. We can stop trying to deal with our health failure alone and start relying on God to help us. We can look to God, and through the eyes of faith we can anticipate that he will eventually deliver us from our present plight. In some cases the deliverance will involve restoration to health. In other cases it will involve helping us to cope with infirmity. Eventually for all of us who have the hope of Christ, it will mean a deliverance into a glorious eternal existence.

A retired Christian businessman entered the hospital for what he expected to be routine surgery. Instead the surgeon found inoperable cancer. Upon being informed of his condition, the patient quite naturally experienced deep disappointment and sorrow at first. A few days later, however, he gently patted his wife's hand. "Don't worry, honey," he said. "I'm in good hands, whatever happens. You can trust God to take good care of me."

Saltness in a Christian can involve setting a good example of faith at a time when health has already failed. It can be knowing that one's earthly days are numbered, but rejoicing in the sure promise that the days of the "life after life" have no end.

Psalm 79

¹O God, the heathen are come into thine inheritance; thy holy temple have they defiled; they have laid Jerusalem on heaps.

²The dead bodies of thy servants have they given to be meat unto the fowls of the heaven, the flesh of thy saints unto the beasts of the earth.

. . . .

⁴We are become a reproach to our neighbours, a scorn and derision to them that are round about us.

⁵How long, Lord? wilt thou be angry for ever? shall thy jealousy burn like fire?

. . . .

⁸O remember not against us former iniquities: let thy tender mercies speedily prevent us: for we are brought very low.

⁹Help us, O God of our salvation, for the

glory of thy name: and deliver us, and purge away our sins, for thy name's sake.

[10]Wherefore should the heathen say, Where is their God? let him be known among the heathen in our sight by the revenging of the blood of thy servants which is shed.

[11]Let the sighing of the prisoner come before thee; according to the greatness of thy power preserve thou those that are appointed to die;

. . . .

[13]So we thy people and sheep of thy pasture will give thee thanks for ever: we will shew forth thy praise to all generations.

The first two psalms that we studied in this chapter related mainly to personal failure: spiritual failure of the individual (sin) and physical failure (ill health). Psalm 79 deals with a third type of failure that had more widespread significance. It was national failure.

National failure, in whatever form it takes, causes stress on its citizenry. In a special way, however, national failure became traumatic for the ancient nations of Israel and Judah. These citizens had unusually strong national ties. As individuals they identified closely with the problems of the whole nation. They grieved over national defeat privately and corporately. In addition, these nations recognized themselves as God's chosen people. Therefore, when they experienced national defeat, they felt that in the eyes of other nations, the Lord's honor was at stake.

Psalm 79 illustrates national lament over defeat. The psalmist wrote it at a time when the nation had experienced extreme failure from a military standpoint. The psalmist does not identify the exact historical event to which he refers. However, because of the descriptions contained in Psalm 79, some scholars believe that the psalm originally related to the destruction of Jerusalem by the Babylonians in 587 BC. Israel later used the psalm in services commemorating the destruction of both the first and second Temples.

As Psalm 79 opens, we find the horrified worshiper pouring out his grief to God over the terrible events that have happened. The descriptions tumble out in quick succession as he assesses the defeat his nation has suffered.

"O God, the heathen have come . . . they have defiled thy holy temple; they have laid Jerusalem in ruins" (v. 1, RSV), he cries. The tone not only reflects grief but also righteous indignation. Heathens have invaded the land, desecrating the Temple and leaving Jerusalem in ruins. They have massacred God's covenant people. Furthermore, they have ritually defiled the city by leaving the dead bodies unburied. These bodies have provided food for fowls and beasts. In the meantime the nation has become the laughing stock of its neighbors (vv. 2-4).

At this point, the thoughts of the righteous man shift from the fact of national defeat to the reason for it. He still directs his words to the Lord, but from a different perspective. Apparently he believes that God allowed this military defeat to occur in order to punish his people for some previous sin. The worshiper passionately pleads that God will change the direction of his wrath from his covenant people to the nations who have defiled his Temple and killed his servants. However, the righteous man does not base his plea on the innocence of God's people, but rather on the tender mercies of the Lord (vv. 5-8).

Verses 9-12 illustrate a point made earlier in this psalm-study. Israel and Judah believed that their defeats cast a bad reflection on the power of the Lord. Their victors would think that if God were powerful, he would have delivered his people instead of letting them suffer defeat. Note in verse 9, however, that the righteous man attributes that interpretation to his enemies, not to his own people. He personally calls the Lord "O God of our salvation" (v. 9).

In verses 11-12, the worshiper makes two petitions. The first one is a request that God use his power to deliver the prisoners exiled in the conquest. The second one is a request for God to defend his own status by reproaching those who have massacred his people. He desires that both the Lord's honor and his people's honor be restored in the sight of ungodly nations.

The righteous man of the Psalter concludes his prayer with a reaffirmation of the faith that he and his nation have in God. Even though his nation has met defeat, his fellow countrymen have been slaughtered and dishonored, and the holy Temple has been defiled by enemies, the salty worshiper still trusts the Lord. He anticipates God's help as though it has already come. Speaking of the future restoration, the worshiper concludes his prayer by pledging: "*Then* we thy people, the flock of thy pasture,/will give thanks to thee for ever;/from generation to generation/we will recount thy praise" (v. 13, RSV).

With the exception of war veterans who served in battle zones, most modern Americans cannot conceive of the kind of defeat described in Psalm 79—cities in ruin, people massacred, and worship centers desecrated. However, our generation has witnessed national failures in other forms: severe economic instability, corruption in government, crises in international relations, and a breakdown in moral and spiritual fiber throughout the nation. How should worshipers of today respond to signs of national failure?

The psalmist sets an example worthy of notice. In the face of disaster he turned to the one source who could give him help—the Lord. He poured out his heart in grief to God, but he did not end his prayer there. Even though he felt that God had allowed this devastation to come upon his people, he reaffirmed his trust in God. In faith he looked forward to the time when God would restore his defeated nation, thanking and praising God because of it.

Should the "salt" of the Christian era do any less?

Chapter 8
The Righteous Man
Participates in Government

Psalm 18

[1]I will love thee, O Lord, my strength.

[2]The Lord is my rock, and my fortress, and my deliverer; my God, my strength, in whom I will trust; my buckler, and the horn of my salvation, and my high tower.

[3]I will call upon the Lord, who is worthy to be praised: so shall I be saved from mine enemies.

. . . .

[32]It is God that girdeth me with strength, and maketh my way perfect.

[33]He maketh my feet like hinds' feet, and setteth me upon my high places.

[34]He teacheth my hands to war, so that a bow of steel is broken by mine arms.

. . . .

[49]Therefore will I give thanks unto thee, O Lord, among the heathen, and sing praises unto thy name.

[50]Great deliverance giveth he to his king; and sheweth mercy to his anointed, to David, and to his seed for evermore.

Certain psalms within the Psalter are designated as "Royal Psalms" because they are associated with the rulers of Israel. In this chapter we shall study three examples of that type of psalm: Psalms 18, 21, and 110.

Sometimes people of today say that "politics and religion don't mix." The psalmist would strongly deny this statement. As a matter of fact, religion and government became very closely intertwined in ancient Israel. Israel viewed the nation's kings as God's representatives on earth. Although many of the kings proved deficient, the kings were, ideally, to seek God's guidance in all their decisions, including military matters, and to reign righteously. They were to be the worship leaders of their people.

Then, as now, a person in high office faced many temptations. One of them was that of becoming intoxicated with his own power. King David, in spite of some of his failings, exemplified how a righteous man in government can honor God instead of self. His thankfulness to God, his remembrance of God's part in his success, and his role of spiritual leadership show that David acted as "salt" in his day.

Psalm 18 is a refreshing example of how a righteous man can participate in government without compromising his faith. The psalm-prayer of King David contains his testimony about the greatness of God. It credits the Lord for making David what he later became, a strong and powerful king and a victorious military leader.

The prayer begins with a tender expression of the righteous king's feeling about God (v. 1). The king's sincerity shines through as he expresses his love for God, his strength. The law "Thou shalt love the Lord thy God" (Deut. 6:5) was basic to all Israel's faith, but the psalmist's spontaneous expression of love in verse 1 suggests more than mere duty. It springs from the innermost part of the worshiper's being.

Unlike many people in high office who consider themselves self-made and self-reliant, the righteous king confesses his dependence on God (v. 2). He calls God his rock (unchangeable source of strength), his fortress (stronghold), and his deliverer. He feels secure, trusting in the Lord. The terms *buckler, horn of my salvation,* and *high tower* are additional terms used by the psalmist to express God's strength.

Because of God's proven faithfulness and power, the righteous king knows that he can always call upon him for help (v. 3). The next few verses illustrate the way in which the Lord can rescue his people from the most dire circumstances.

Due to the length of Psalm 18 (50 verses), only selected verses can be discussed in this brief commentary. In general, however, verses 7-15 deal with God's manifestation of his might in the forces of nature. Verses 16-19 relate to God's deliverance of the king from his enemies. Verses 20-24 discuss the Lord's reward to the king for his righteousness. Verses 25-30 show the connection between man's attitude toward God and God's dealings with man. The unifying factor in all of these segments is the focus on God as the source of the king's and nation's strength and blessing.

Verses 32-34 continue to reveal the humility of the righteous king. The king again asserts that his power comes from God, not from himself. God girds him with strength. He removes the barriers ("maketh my way perfect," v. 32) so that nothing will block the path of David's kingship. The Lord enables the king to be fleetfooted like a hind, an important ability during ancient warfare. He sets the righteous king on a mountain stronghold where the king can safely oversee his kingdom (v. 33). Furthermore, the Lord trains him in the military arts, strengthening David's arms.

In verses 34-48, the righteous king recalls the sweet victory he has tasted as a result of God's ever present help. Israel's enemies learned to fear David because of his success, even bringing gifts to him to keep themselves in his favor.

The prayer-psalm ends on a note of thanksgiving (vv. 49-50). The righteous king gratefully expresses his thanksgiving to the Lord. In the presence of the nations around him, he thanks and praises God for what God has done for and through him. The righteous king does not say, "I made possible my own deliverance." Rather, he says, "Great deliverance giveth he (God) to his king; and sheweth mercy to his anointed, to David, and to his seed for evermore" (v. 50).

Today, in some respects, each of us participates in government whether we serve in an office or not. We have the privilege of voting for candidates whom we feel will represent our people well. We also have the right to let our voices be heard on issues and legislation that can contribute to good government.

However, an elected official has a special duty to serve in an honest and responsible manner. Good leadership, both local and national, can profoundly affect the moral and ethical climate of the city, state, and nation.

In a recent political campaign, one of the candidates had the reputation of being a rather idealistic young man with high moral scruples. At a political rally shortly after the young man's candidacy had been announced, a seasoned voter listened with interest, then approached the candidate with a query. "I just want to ask one question," said the voter. "What is a nice guy like you doing, running for political office?"

Unfortunately, the "nice guy" in government frequently either gets "clobbered" or gradually compromises his principles. The temptations and pressures of serving in a high political office can be severe. The man who emerges from office with his moral and religious scruples still intact, and who can still humbly recognize God's role in his life, is truly "salt" in his nation.

Psalm 21

¹The king shall joy in thy strength, O Lord; and in thy salvation how greatly shall he rejoice!

²Thou hast given him his heart's desire, and hast not withholden the request of his lips. Selah.

. . . .

⁴He asked life of thee, and thou gavest it him, even length of days for ever and ever.

⁵His glory is great in thy salvation: honour and majesty hast thou laid upon him.

. . . .

⁷For the king trusteth in the Lord, and through the mercy of the most High he shall not be moved.

⁸Thine hand shall find out all thine enemies: thy right hand shall find out those that hate thee.

. . . .

¹²Therefore shalt thou make them turn

**their back, when thou shalt make ready
thine arrows upon thy strings against the
face of them.**

**[13]Be thou exalted, Lord, in thine own
strength: so will we sing and praise thy
power.**

We commonly use the expression "getting off on the right
foot" to describe the advantage of making a favorable start.
Whether a person is just beginning a new job or being in-
stalled into office, he or she wants to begin on the right foot-
ing.

In ancient Israel the coronation ceremonies that accompanied the crowning of a king helped the king to get off to a
good start in his reign. Since the king served as both a political and religious figure, he and his fellow countrymen attached great importance to the religious aspect of his reign.
The coronation took place in the sanctuary and included
prayers of dedication, supplication, trust, and intercession.
Even the feast that followed the coronation was called the
"feast of Yahweh" (Jehovah).

Psalm 21 was one of the coronation hymns used in the
crowning of the king. Throughout the psalm we see evidence of faith in God, thanksgiving, praise, and desire to
exalt God. Psalm 21 portrays the king foremost as one who
trusts the Lord.

As the psalm begins, the priest offers a prayer concerning
the newly crowned king. His prayer serves two purposes. (1)
It expresses gratitude to God for what he has done for the
king—the support, blessing, and approval of the king that
God has already shown. (2) It reminds the king of his religious duty and of the debt of gratitude he owes the Lord for
making him what he has become.

First, the priest reassures God that the king rejoices in the Lord's power and in his deliverance. The priest recalls how the Lord provided for the king's desire and answered his prayer (vv. 1-2). In the King James Version, verse 3 uses a word that has a different meaning today. The word *preventest* originally meant "comes to meet." Therefore, what verse 3 means is that the Lord himself is present at this ceremony. God has come on the occasion to give his divine blessing on the king and to participate in the coronation.

Continuing the prayer, the priest marvels at how the king asked for God's blessing of long life and God gave him this assurance. "For ever and ever" (v. 4) does not imply an immortal existence. It carries the idea of the more modern expression "long live the king!" The Israelites associated long life with God's favor. Because of an Israelite king's unique political-religious status, long life carried special meaning. The king's life span had particular importance because he held the status of God's anointed one. (See 2 Sam. 1:13-17 for an example of this concept.)

The priest moves on in the prayer by referring to three qualities that God gives the king: glory, honor, and majesty. These are the qualities also associated with the heavenly King. As God's earthly representative, the king would reflect these qualities. Furthermore, the Lord would bless him and issue blessings through him. The king would rejoice in God's presence and fellowship (vv. 5-6).

Next, the priest focuses on the basis of the blessings received by the king: "For the king trusteth in the Lord" (v. 7). No matter how good a military leader he was or what other attributes he had, the king would fail without God's help. So long as he trusted in the Lord, however, he would continue to receive God's blessing.

Verses 8-12 present somewhat of a problem. They seem to shift from a prayer to God to a blessing pronounced on the king. If the verses are still part of the prayer, they serve as an affirmation of God's power to destroy the king's enemies. If, however, the verses are a blessing on the king, the priest must be reassuring the king that God will give him victory. In either instance, ideally the king's enemies and God's enemies would be the same.

The concluding verse of Psalm 21 takes the form of a prayer entered into by the whole congregation. The worshipers have had the privilege of witnessing the making of history in the coronation of their king. Their reverential awe and their awareness of God's covenant relationship with Israel has also been renewed. Appropriately, therefore, they conclude the hymn-prayer used in the coronation of their earthly king with words of praise for their heavenly King: "Be thou exalted, Lord, in thine own strength: so will we sing and praise thy power" (v. 13).

In summary, a righteous participant in government becomes salt by setting a worthy example for his people. He begins by acknowledging God's gracious gifts to him and continues by dedicating himself to uphold godly principles in public office. He seeks God's guidance and help in the ruling of his people. He demonstrates more interest in exalting God than in exalting himself. The heart of the matter is that no matter what his rank or office may be, a good leader trusts God for help.

Persons of today have a responsibility to support candidates who trust God, but who do not merely attend church as a means of getting votes. We also have the responsibility of praying for our elected officials, just as the ancient worshipers prayed for the new king—through prayers of dedication, supplication, and intercession.

Saltness, whether serving personally in public office or in selecting and supporting those who do, involves upholding righteous leadership and leading other people to do likewise.

Psalm 110

¹The Lord said unto my Lord, Sit thou at my right hand, until I make thine enemies thy footstool.

²The Lord shall send the rod of thy strength out of Zion: rule thou in the midst of thine enemies.

³Thy people shall be willing in the day of thy power, in the beauties of holiness from the womb of the morning: thou hast the dew of thy youth.

⁴The Lord hath sworn, and will not repent, Thou art a priest for ever after the order of Melchizedek.

⁵The Lord at thy right hand shall strike through kings in the day of his wrath.

⁶He shall judge among the heathen, he shall fill the places with the dead bodies; he shall wound the heads over many countries.

⁷He shall drink of the brook in the way: therefore shall he lift up the head.

We have already studied two examples from the Psalter illustrating righteous leadership in high office. First, through the study of Psalm 18 we focused on the importance of refusing to compromise moral and ethical principles for the sake of political expediency. Second, through the study of Psalm 21 we recalled the religious duty of upholding and praying for high leaders who trust God. In studying these

two psalms we saw a glimmer of the saltness recommended
by Christ centuries later.

Psalm 110, our third example of righteous participation in
government, goes beyond a mere glimmer of Christ's kind
of saltness, however. Although originally written to describe
a righteous political king, Psalm 110 clearly found ultimate
fulfillment in the advent of Christ. New Testament quotations from the psalm appear in Matthew 22:44; Acts 2:34; 1
Corinthians 15:25; Ephesians 1:20, and Hebrews 1:3, 13.

In studying this psalm we again need to keep in mind the
duty of Israelite kings to be the worship leaders of their
people. The title "A Priestly King" is therefore an appropriate one for Psalm 110. The first four verses comprise divine
oracles delivered to the king; the remainder of the psalm, a
prophecy relating to the king. The main emphasis in the
psalm lies in the king's role as a spiritual leader of Israel.

As indicated above, the opening words of Psalm 110 are
familiar to us because of their quotation and application in
the New Testament. However, the words applied more
immediately to the king being enthroned in ancient Israel.

The speaker begins by voicing the divine oracle that God
had laid upon his heart and mind to deliver. "The Lord said
unto my Lord, Sit thou at my right hand, until I make thine
enemies thy footstool" (v. 1). In verse 1, "*the* Lord" refers to
God; "*my* Lord" refers to the king.

People of the ancient world coveted the position of sitting
at the right hand of one in authority. Israelites joined the
Arabians, Greeks, and Egyptians in longing for that honor.
Thus, the Lord's invitation to the king of Israel to sit at his
right hand (v. 1) implied a status of authority and respect.
Such a status would assure the king of a victorious reign
("until I make thine enemies thy footstool").

A righteous king would understand that this honor implied a responsibility. Just as the people recognized the

king's authority, so the king recognized God's authority. Not only had the Lord made possible the king's status, he would also enable the king to rule in the midst of enemies (v. 2).

The king receives a further promise that in times of war his subjects will willingly serve (v. 3). The people of Israel viewed military service in wartime as a religious duty. Israel based this view on the religious significance of Israelite king-ship and on the fact that the king was also a military figure. Verse 3 contains the reassurance that the king could depend on the finest young men of the land to volunteer their service. The figure of morning dew describes the vital-ity of the young men who would serve.

Although implied elsewhere, the king's sacred duty of serving as religious leader appears most clearly in verse 4. God's purpose from early times had been that Israel's kings would be worship leaders. The king was not to separate the religious and political aspects of kingship. The Lord had not, and would not, change his mind ("repent") concerning the matter, even though the sinful nature of humanity might temporarily thwart the divine purpose. Israel's kings were to follow the pattern of Melchizedek, an ancient royal priest, who merged political and worship leadership. God ex-pected the kings to mediate between God and Israel and to lead Israel to act like a holy nation.

Verses 5-7 take the form of a prophecy relating to the king. The essence of these verses is that the Lord will be with the king, fighting his battles for him and with him. Israel could look forward to the day when God would destroy Israel's enemies ("the day of his wrath," v. 5). In that day God's judgment would fall upon the heathen. The psalm ends with an instruction to the king to "drink of the brook" (v. 7), possibly a symbolic act representing refreshment and new strength.

Psalm 110 portrays the righteous king, ideally, as one

who served a priestly function with his nation. Although figuratively honored by being invited to sit at the right hand of God, the king recognized God's graciousness, not his own worthiness, as the reason for the honor. The righteous participant in government looked upon kingship as a sacred office. Because of his religious responsibility, he had God's promise of a victorious reign.

Christians recognize Jesus Christ as the ultimate fulfillment of the ideal king described in Psalm 110. He became a spiritual king in the deepest meaning of the words—a priestly king, yet King of kings. After his resurrection, "he was received up into heaven, and sat on the right hand of God" (Mark 16:19).

Under Christ's direction, Christians become part of the "holy and . . . royal priesthood" (1 Peter 2:5, 9) today. Our own priesthood unfolds as we offer up our "spiritual sacrifices" to God. The sacrifices may be ones of praise, material offerings, thanksgiving, and righteous living (Heb. 13:15-16). The greatest sacrifice we can offer, however, is the example of a life dedicated to his service. The ancient Israelites salted their sacrifices as a symbolic means of making them more savory to God (Lev. 2:13). Persons of today become *salt upon their sacrificial offering* by presenting lives to God that are holy and righteous (Rom. 12:1).

Chapter 9
The Righteous Man
Communes with God

Psalm 145

[1]I will extol thee, my God, O king; and I will bless thy name for ever and ever.

[2]Every day will I bless thee; and I will praise thy name for ever and ever.

[3]Great is the Lord, and greatly to be praised; and his greatness is unsearchable.

. . . .

[8]The Lord is gracious, and full of compassion; slow to anger, and of great mercy.

[9]The Lord is good to all: and his tender mercies are over all his works.

[10]All thy works shall praise thee, O Lord; and thy saints shall bless thee.

. . . .

[17]The Lord is righteous in all his ways, and holy in all his works.

[18]The Lord is nigh unto all them that call upon him, to all that call upon him in truth.

. . . .

[21]My mouth shall speak the praise of the Lord: and let all flesh bless his holy name for ever and ever.

A worshiper commented about his pastor, "I appreciate and am inspired by my pastor's sermons; they are excellent. Even more, however, I am uplifted by his prayer in the Sunday morning worship services. He obviously spends a great deal of time preparing to lead us in an experience of true communion with the Lord."

If we could overhear the innermost prayers of other persons very often, we might learn much about those persons. We could learn of their concerns, to what measure they depended on God for guidance, and get some clues about the depth of their commitment to the Lord. In brief, we could know something of the saltness of their worship example and leadership, as the worshiper did his pastor's.

The psalmist invites us to do that very thing. He allows us to eavesdrop as he communes with God; in fact, he invites his fellow worshipers to join him. As a mortal being, this righteous man of the Psalter runs the gamut of human experiences—good and bad, inspiring and less than savory. In this section, three types of prayers are exemplified: words of praise, prayers of penitence, and expressions of thanksgiving. A portion of Psalm 145, printed above, will serve as an example of his inspirational prayer of praise.

In Psalm 145 the righteous man speaks not only for himself, but also for the covenant community he represents. This prayer-psalm likely served as part of the ritual at the feast of the covenant. At that feast, the kingship of God had a major emphasis.

Verses 1-3 provide us with a clue that the occasion may have been the type of feast mentioned above. The psalmist addresses God as a king (v. 1). Before Israel established an earthly monarchy, she already had a king (the Lord). After the monarchy began, the earthly king was only to serve as a representative of the heavenly King. In commemoration of God's kingship, Israel had "enthronement" celebrations periodically to serve as a reminder of God's rule.

The righteous man addresses his heavenly monarch with appropriate praise. He recognizes the unsearchable greatness of God and seeks a way to express his adoration. He commits himself to a promise that many of us would dare not make: to praise God every single day of his life (v. 2).

In verses 4-7 the psalmist muses about the areas in which God's greatness shows forth—his mighty acts, majesty, judgment, and righteousness. All of these attributes deserved the worshiper's praise, for they revealed the glory of God. Verses 8-10, however, reveal some qualities of God with which the average worshiper can easily identify. What worshiper has not found comfort and help in knowing that the Lord is a compassionate God, slow to anger and merciful? Who, in fact, has not experienced God's gracious love pouring into his own life? The psalmist does not directly say so, but these qualities probably "struck home" with him even more than the others. All of creation praises God and gives thanks to him in response to his grace, compassion, and mercy (v. 10).

The righteous man of the Psalter goes into more detail in the next few verses about the way God's mercy manifests itself. He speaks of how the Lord helps those who have slipped and satisfies the needs of every living creature. Verse 17 carries the reminder that God is righteous in all his ways and holy in all his works.

The accessibility of God was (and is) an important gift to worshipers. Verse 18, therefore, deals with a blessing near and dear to the heart of the psalmist. He knew from both a positive and negative standpoint what it was like to experience God's nearness. For example, Psalm 32 illustrates how unconfessed sin stood as a barrier between him and God and what relief he felt when he experienced God's nearness again. He also recognized that the Lord is only near to those who approach him with sincerity ("call upon him in truth," Ps. 145:18). Only the person who stands in the right relationship with God can know that God hears his prayer. The Lord preserves those who love him and seek his help.

Psalm 145 ends on a note of joyful praise. The righteous man invites his fellow worshipers to join him in praising God. He views praise as a vital element in the prayer life of both the individual and of the community of believers. Like the "salt" whom Jesus taught to pray centuries later, the psalmist had learned to hallow God's name and to lead his fellow worshipers to do likewise. As he states in verse 21, "Let all flesh bless his holy name for ever and ever." The righteous man had also learned to find joy and cause for thanksgiving in his communion with God. The blending of reverence and praise illustrated by Psalm 145 brings to mind the words of a New Testament writer who said: "Let us offer the sacrifice of praise to God continually" (Heb. 13:15).

Some persons of today never seem to progress in their prayer life beyond the "gimme" prayer of a small child. They turn to God in prayer only when they need or want something. There is a proper time for asking God's help, as the next two psalms will illustrate, and God is accessible at those times. However, the time also comes when we should lay aside our own needs and problems and simply approach God with praise and thanksgiving.

The high rate of income taxes has become a major problem in our country. We have trouble getting into a spirit of thanksgiving when income tax time rolls around. Our inclination, instead, is to pray that something miraculous will happen to prevent our having to pay such high taxes.

A man had been grumbling all week about the tax form he was filling out. On Sunday morning he sarcastically commented that he believed that he would just stay home from church; he really did not have much to praise the Lord for this week. His wife let him "blow off steam" for awhile, then responded calmly: "Just remember, dear, in order to be taxed you have to have an income—and without any income, you might starve to death. Maybe you have more to be thankful for than you realize!"

Do you ever feel sorry for yourself to the extent that you find it hard to pray words of praise and thanksgiving to God? True saltness lies in the ability to praise and thank God in *all* of life's circumstances and to lead others to do it. This trait does not come naturally, but it can be cultivated. More of us need to make our resolution that of the psalmist: "Every day will I bless thee; and I will praise thy name for ever and ever" (Ps. 145:2).

Psalm 51

¹Have mercy upon me, O God, according to thy lovingkindness: according unto the multitude of thy tender mercies blot out my transgressions.

²Wash me thoroughly from mine iniquity, and cleanse me from my sin.

³For I acknowledge my transgressions: and my sin is ever before me.

. . . .

⁷Purge me with hyssop, and I shall be clean: wash me, and I shall be whiter than snow.

. . . .

¹⁰Create in me a clean heart, O God; and renew a right spirit within me.

. . . .

¹⁶For thou desirest not sacrifice; else would I give it: thou delightest not in burnt offering.
¹⁷The sacrifices of God are a broken spirit: a broken and a contrite heart, O God, thou wilt not despise.

Criticism by other people tends to bring out either the worst or best qualities in a person. A basically evil person will respond to it with retaliation, counter-charges, or excuses, no matter how just the criticism is. A basically righteous person, on the other hand, will respond to valid criticism with acknowledgment of guilt and sincere repentance. The psalmist is an example of the latter kind of person, one who sinned, was confronted with his sin, and penitently asked God's forgiveness.

Biblical scholars generally view Psalms 32 and 51 as one unit dealing with the same incident. As indicated earlier in this volume, Psalm 32 contains an account of how the psalmist tried to hide his guilt from God but found relief only when he repented and confessed his sin. Psalm 51 records the essence of David's prayer of penitence, his request for spiritual cleansing, and his recognition of the nature of acceptable sacrifice for sin.

The sin that prompted David's confession was not simply a contrived one, designed to illustrate a point. It involved an infraction of two of the Ten Commandments, adultery and murder. In an effort to cover up an adulterous relationship with Bathsheba (2 Sam. 11), David had arranged for the death of Bathsheba's husband, Uriah. God used a prophet, Nathan, to prick David's conscience by confronting him with the seriousness of his sin. The writer of 2 Samuel makes no attempt to whitewash David's sin.

Nevertheless, the sins described above were not representative of David's life. David was basically a righteous, God-fearing man who made a serious mistake and paid dearly for it. He shows his vulnerability to temptation by the sin he committed, but he illustrates his saltness by his profound grief and public penitence. David's example of repentance and his trust in God's forgiveness became the salt (the preservative factor) that enabled the prophet to reassure him: "The Lord also hath put away thy sin" (2 Sam. 12:13).

Psalm 51 is an example of a very necessary type of prayer in the life of a believer, a prayer of penitence. Not all persons commit the same sins as David, but "all have sinned, and come short of the glory of God" (Rom. 3:23).

The psalm begins with a petition to the Lord to extend mercy. The worshiper does not base his request on his own worthiness or even on the basically righteous nature of his past performance. Rather, he bases his petition on the already proven graciousness of God. In the past, God has shown himself to be both merciful and gracious. The word translated "lovingkindness" (v. 1) is one of the most beautiful and communicative words in the Hebrew language. It relates to the sublime love of God that made possible the covenant between God and Israel. The worshiper dares to ask for God's mercy because he knows the character of the covenant God.

The seriousness of the worshiper's sin has already been discussed. Nevertheless, his case is not hopeless. The greatness of God's mercy exceeds the seriousness of David's sin.

Remembrance of this fact gives the penitent worshiper hope.

The last part of verse 1 and the two clauses in verse 2 describe three methods by which the worshiper's sin can be removed. Each method involves God's gracious help.

First, God can *blot out* the sin. The figure suggests an account book in which the debt is cancelled. The penitent sinner asks God to erase his guilt, just as a compassionate creditor might erase the debt of a person in a hopeless financial strait.

Second, God can thoroughly *wash* the sinner so that the sin no longer exists (v. 2a). Here the psalmist pictures a launderer who "deep cleans" the soiled garment. The sinner wants God to cleanse him spiritually in such a way that he will be both ceremonially and inwardly purified.

Third, God can *cleanse* him in the sense of ritually cleansing a diseased person, such as one who has leprosy. Just as a leper was required to cry out "unclean, unclean!" until he was pronounced clean by the priest, so the sinner bore the stigma of "unclean" until God removed his guilt.

Each of the three methods described for cleansing is followed by three words that describe three types of sin. The psalmist uses the word translated as "trangressions" first. In the Hebrew the term *transgressions* (v. 1) means rebellion against God or defection from him. The word *iniquity* (v. 2) means depraved conduct. The word *sin* (v. 2) carries the idea of missing the mark. All three words combine to describe the plight of the repentant worshiper.

Verses 3-6 contain the psalmist's acknowledgment of his sin against Uriah (Bathsheba's husband). However, he knew that his greatest sin was against God, who forbade murder and adultery. The psalmist recognized, as did Isaiah, that no person could stand up under the scrutiny of the holy God (Isa. 6:5). The tendency toward sin is an inborn trait. God desires that man be inwardly pure, a feat attainable with God's help in overcoming man's natural bent toward sin.

Recognizing this need for God's help in removing his guilt, the psalmist appeals to God. He implores in verse 7, "Purge me with hyssop" (an herb used in the rite of cleansing one afflicted with leprosy). As in verse 2, he seems to draw a comparison in verse 7 between leprosy and sin. Again, in faith, he adds: "Wash me, and I shall be whiter than snow" (symbol of purity).

Verses 8-9 contain a continued prayer for healing the "bones which thou hast broken" (a reference to how shattered he was because of the breach between him and God). Throughout the psalm the writer assumes responsibility for the guilt that caused this breach.

The psalmist had already acknowledged his personal sin (v. 3). He had also commented on his tendency toward sin as an inborn human trait (v. 5). These statements form the background for his request in verse 10: "Create in me a clean heart, O God; and renew a right spirit within me." Both because he was part of sinful humanity and because of his personal guilt, he needed a spiritual re-creation.

The whole prayer reflects the worshiper's desire to feel God's nearness again. Verses 11-12 repeat that thought. Without a consciousness of God's presence he can have neither joy nor the assurance that God will strengthen and uphold him. As soon as the sinner has been restored, he will instruct other sinners about God's grace and show them how to return to God (v. 13).

In verses 14-15 the psalmist returns to his own case. He asks God to deliver him from punishment by death ("blood guiltiness") for the crimes he has committed—murder and adultery. If the Lord will but "open his lips" (let him join in congregational worship worthily again), the psalmist will respond by praising him.

Verses 16-17 are two very familiar verses, but especially verse 17. The psalmist showed spiritual insight beyond most persons of his day. Like Amos, he recognized that sacrificial offerings on the altar were meaningless if not accompanied by a righteous life (Amos 5:21-24). If burnt offerings alone would have satisfied God, the worshiper would gladly have given them. The worshiper knew, however, that the Lord would not grant him forgiveness purely on the basis of material sacrifices. God desired a different kind of sacrifice: a broken spirit and contrite heart (penitence and humility), a life submitted to God.

The psalm closes with a plea in behalf of the nation. Due to its reference to the building of the walls of Jerusalem (v. 18), this portion may have been added on by exiles before the rebuilding of Jerusalem and the Temple.

The basically righteous man portrayed in Psalm 51 had committed a grave sin. By his admission, his hope for restoration lay in God's mercy, not his own merit. Nevertheless, his profound grief over his sin, and his spirit of deep repentance, became a salty example for other transgressors to follow.

Before we criticize the psalmist for his outrageous conduct when he should have known better, let us reexamine our own lives. Who of us has not fallen short of the mark of righteousness, even though we really know better? Who can truthfully say, "I have never needed God's forgiveness"?

An acquaintance of mine becomes greatly incensed when she hears someone say of Christians in general, "We are *all* only sinners saved by grace." This indignant lady honestly feels that she has never sinned and does not even want to be assigned to the category of a "*saved* sinner." She will offer prayers of thanksgiving, but she sees no need of expressing penitence or asking forgiveness for any reason.

To confess guilt where guilt does not exist is shallow. However, to refuse to acknowledge sin where sin does exist is even more shallow. The excuses we make for our sins and our refusal to acknowledge our sins only make things worse. The writer of 1 John states the situation clearly: "If we say that we have no sin, we deceive ourselves ... if we confess our sins, he is faithful and just to forgive us" (1 John 1:8-9).

The salty worshiper of today, then, is the one who acknowledges guilt where it exists, shows a spirit of sincere repentance, and asks for God's gracious forgiveness.

Psalm 136

¹**O give thanks unto the Lord; for he is good: for his mercy endureth for ever.**

. . . .

⁴**To him who alone doeth great wonders: for his mercy endureth for ever.**
⁵**To him that by wisdom made the heavens: for his mercy endureth for ever.**

. . . .

¹³**To him which divided the Red sea into parts: for his mercy endureth for ever:**

. . . .

²³**Who remembered us in our low estate: for his mercy endureth for ever:**
²⁴**And hath redeemed us from our enemies: for his mercy endureth for ever.**

²⁵**Who giveth food to all flesh: for his mercy endureth for ever.**
²⁶**O give thanks unto the God of heaven: for his mercy endureth for ever.**

In this chapter we have already noted two types of prayer commonly used in the psalmist's day: prayers of praise and penitential prayers. Other types could be cited: prayers for the welfare of the nation, the wisdom and success of the king, laments to God, expressions of trust, requests for healing or victory, and even pleas for the destruction of enemies. It seems fitting, however, to conclude the chapter with an example of prayer in one of its noblest forms, that of thanksgiving. Prayers of thanksgiving join those of praise in representing communication with God at its highest level.

Psalm 136, one of many examples of thanksgiving prayers in the Psalter, was used as an antiphonal prayer hymn. The choir would chant the first half of the verse, then the congregation would chant the second. The exact festival time at which the hymn was used by Israel is uncertain. It may have been at the harvest festival, but it could also have been used at the Passover or new year festival. The psalm is of post-exilic origin.

The person I have designated as the "righteous man" has served as a representative of all true worshipers of his day. That fact makes it especially appropriate for the concluding psalm in the study to be one in which all Israel obviously participated. The Jews commonly referred to Psalm 136 as the "Great Hallel" (hallelujah).

The three opening antiphonal verses contain an appeal for all Israel to give thanks to the Lord. The basis of the appeal is the goodness of God whose mercy endures forever. The remainder of Psalm 136 deals with many reasons why Israel should express gratitude to the Lord. The righteous man, as a representative of every true worshiper of his day, looks to this festival celebration as a time to recall and to give thanks.

The righteous man first reflects on the magnificent works of creation (vv. 4-9). Who, but God, could perform these great wonders? Only the omnipotent God could make the heavens (v. 5), stretch out the earth upon the waters (v. 6), and create the great lights (sun, moon, and stars) that illumine the universe. The Genesis 1 account of creation is deeply integrated into the worshiper's thought pattern. As he considers each of the evidences of God's creative power, he remembers God's enduring mercy.

The thoughts of the righteous man then turn to God's great acts of deliverance (vv. 10-15). The worshiper recalls gratefully the story of how the Lord became Israel's champion in Egypt. Very likely, his grandfather and father had retold the story to him many times, just as it had been retold to them.

He recalls from the Exodus and Deuteronomy narratives how the Lord proved his power over the strength of Pharaoh and divided the Red Sea so that his people could escape (vv. 12-15). After a recitation of each of these wondrous acts of God, the worshiper is prompted to comment: "For his mercy endureth forever."

Next, the mind of the righteous man focuses on the culmination of the deliverance from Egypt and the wilderness journey—Israel's arrival at the Promised Land (vv. 16-22). The story of God's protection of the people in the wilderness and his provision of manna for them has become well-known to us. However, we sometimes overlook the reference made in verses 17-20 to God's smiting of great kings. The Promised Land (Canaan) was already occupied by other nations when Israel arrived. Therefore, Israel had to conquer the inhabitants of the territory before settling it. Throughout this process God had reassured Israel that he would fight for Israel (Ex. 14:14 and Deut. 3:22). As always, God kept his promise. Verses 19-20 list two kings God had enabled Israel to conquer. The enduring mercy of God, who had made the victories possible, remains the refrain of the righteous man throughout verses 16-22.

Verses 23-24 may be another reference to Israel's former enslavement in Egypt. Certainly enslavement would put *any* persons in "low estate" (v. 23). However, the psalmist could just as easily have been referring to Israel's plight, as a struggling and disunited people, faced with the prospects of fighting to occupy Canaan. In either case, the point is that God recognized the low estate of his people and helped them. The righteous man remembers the history of how God "redeemed us from our enemies" (v. 24). He again feels inspired to say of God, "His mercy endureth for ever."

The worshiper's prayer of thanksgiving ends with a reference to God's provision of sustenance for those whom he has created (vv. 25-26). If Psalm 136 was used at the harvest festival, as some scholars believe, verses 25-26 form an especially fitting conclusion for the prayer hymn. This festival would bring to mind God's part in making the harvest of food possible. The God who created the universe, delivered his people from captivity, led and sustained them in the wilderness, and helped them occupy Canaan, would continue to provide for them. The righteous man concludes his meditation with the refrain that has run from the beginning of his prayer to the end, that of the enduring mercy of God.

The representative "righteous man" of the Psalter showed his saltness in his testimonial prayer of thanksgiving to God. His enthusiastic response to God's gracious acts, and his joyous expressions of thanksgiving, had a zestful influence on the community. Psalm 136 began by serving as one man's testimony of God's works and of his gratitude for them. It later became the thankful prayer of a whole nation over a long expanse of time.

We have all heard that a little salt can go a long way. The salty example and leadership of the psalmist shows this fact to be true. His devotional prayer life has had an impact throughout the centuries on the lives of both Jews and Christians.

As "salt" in today's world, Christians have an opportunity to let our seasoning be felt a long way, too. We can begin by setting an example of gratitude toward God at home and at church, and by letting our appreciation for God's gracious care be known throughout the community.

We have already noted the theme that runs through Psalm 136. It is: "O give thanks unto the Lord; for he is good: for his mercy endureth for ever." If the righteous man of the Psalter had cause to give continuous thanks, think how much more reason Christians have to express gratitude to God! Various New Testament writers expressed a similar thought, but the writer of a letter to the church of the Thessalonians summed it up most succinctly. He supported the view of the psalmist but expanded it to include the added dimension that Christ gives. It is appropriate to close this study of Psalm 136 with the Christian concept of the psalmist's exhortation: "In every thing give thanks: for this is the will of God in Christ Jesus concerning you" (1 Thess. 5:18).

Summary

Throughout this study of the Psalms, we have seen numerous evidences that the "righteous man of the Psalter" (representative of the true worshiper) became salt in his own day. The responses he made to the varied experiences of life, although confined to the light of the Old Testament, nevertheless reflected a preservative and zestful influence. As indicated in the introduction, he was a forerunner of the type of worshiper whom Christ later referred to as "salt" (Matt. 5:13).

Chapter 1 gave us a view of how the righteous man of the Psalter assessed happiness. A study of Psalm 1 showed that he looked, both negatively and positively, for the source of true happiness. He found it in obedience toward God. The righteous man then considered how happiness manifests itself (Ps. 128). He concluded that work, family, and nation can be great sources of blessing and happiness. Psalm 84, the last psalm discussed in that chapter, focused on the special source of happiness he found in the experience of worship. In assessing happiness the worshiper had shown his saltness by looking for happiness from a spiritual standpoint and by rejoicing over the right things in the right manner.

Chapter 2 dealt with the way the righteous man faced affliction. Psalm 3 illustrated how he faced affliction within a family—the plot of his own son against him. His undaunted faith in this hurtful experience exemplified saltness for all generations. Psalm 69 illustrated how he dealt with enemies outside the family unit. Although he lived by the standards of his own day, rather than by Christ's standards, he worked through his bitterness and emerged as a thankful worshiper. Psalm 10 related to the "why?" of affliction, a problem with which many people of our own day must wrestle. The righteous man concluded that ultimately God will balance the scales of justice. Psalms 3, 69, and 10 demonstrated his saltness in trusting God in spite of affliction.

Chapter 3 provided us a glimpse of how the righteous man exulted in faith. The psalms used here are only three of many that could have been used to illustrate the inspiring faith of the worshiper. Psalm 23 focused on the righteous man's faith that God was both a good shepherd and a gracious host. The emphasis in Psalm 46 lay in the worshiper's view of God as an ever present refuge and strength. Psalm 27:1-6 communicated the faith that enabled the righteous man to deal with life-threatening problems. The saltness of this worshiper became apparent in his personal example of faith that served as a pattern for the community.

Chapter 4 focused on the way that the righteous man coped with that enemy of all of us—doubt. Psalm 77 realistically illustrated that even a righteous man can have temporary times of doubt, but he can move from doubt to faith. Psalm 22, from which Jesus quoted on the cross, showed how suffering can affect a person of faith. It revealed that the righteous man eventually recognized that God could do for him what he could not do for himself—lift him from his mental anguish. Psalm 13 portrayed the righteous man as one who discovered that light lies beyond the shadows of life. All three psalms point to the worshiper as one whose salt never really lost its savor in spite of times of doubt.

Chapter 5 took a look at how the righteous man of the

Psalter interpreted nature. Psalm 19:1-6 focused on the worshiper's view of heaven and earth as a general witness to God's creativity. It spoke of how the heavens were continuously declaring the glory of God and how the firmament showed God's genius. Psalm 29 expressed the view that the source of the power of nature was in God—the Lord was God of the storms, as well as God of his people. Psalm 8, more specifically than Psalm 19, discussed the role of nature in witnessing to God's glory. However, all three psalms demonstrated the righteous man's salty witness to the covenant community that nature is marvelous because God made it that way.

Chapter 6 invited us to see how the righteous man of the Psalter responded to success. Psalm 66 illustrated the proper response to success on three levels: international, national, and personal. The psalm emphasized thanksgiving to God as a worthy response. Psalm 67 dealt with success both in regard to harvest and spiritual matters. It took into account the place of other nations in God's plan and summoned other nations to acknowledge God's power. Psalm 124 related to military success and frankly gave credit to God for Israel's victory. It began, however, with personal acknowledgment of God's part in the success and moved on to a summons to all Israel to do likewise. Each of these psalms illustrates saltness in the example of thanksgiving and praise to God as the proper responses to success.

Chapter 7 dealt with a topic most of us would rather forget, that of failure. It openly and frankly approached the problem of failure and showed how the righteous man contended with it. Psalm 32 focused on sin as a significant form of failure. It emphasized the importance of repentance and of confession of sin to God. Psalm 38 presented the view that all failure, including that of health, was in some way related to sin and that only God's forgiveness could correct it. Psalm 79, the last example in the chapter, depicted how the righteous man led his community in contending properly with national failure. In these psalms the righteous man became salt by personally accepting responsibility for his own sin and leading his nation to do likewise. The responses he recommended for the failure that we call "sin" were the ones later set forth by Christ: repentance, confession, and the asking of God's forgiveness.

Chapter 8 provided insights on how the righteous man of the Psalter participated in government. The psalms selected for discussion in this chapter fall into the category of "royal psalms." Psalm 18 showed how a righteous man participated in government without compromising his faith. Psalm 21, a coronation hymn, illustrated the emphasis on religion in enthronement ceremonies. Psalm 110 dwelt on the priestly function of a king in ancient Israel. We called attention to the ultimate fulfillment of the ideal "priest king" in Christ Jesus. The salt of the ancient worshiper, as he participated in government, was shown in three respects: his righteous leadership, his expressed dependence on God's help, and his duty to represent God well.

Chapter 9, the concluding Psalter discussion, dealt with worship—how the righteous man communed with God. The psalms chosen for inclusion in this chapter illustrated three types of prayers offered by the true worshiper. Psalm 145 contained a joyous prayer of praise to the Lord. Psalm 51 illustrated a prayer of penitence. Appropriately, Psalm 136, the final psalm discussed in this book, was one of thanksgiving. The three prayer elements represented by these psalms are reemphasized many times throughout the New Testament. They provide a salty example for worshipers of every generation to follow as part of their communion with God.

In summary, the righteous man of the Psalter represented

the true worshiper in every generation. In the varied experiences of his life, he demonstrated the qualities that Christ set forth for his own disciples: praise and thanksgiving to God, penitence for sin, faith that looks beyond present anguish, desire for God's guidance, good works, right interpretation of happiness and worship, and the proper response to success.

Our Lord Jesus himself quoted from the Psalter, as did the apostles. The Psalter contains messianic references. The early church attached great significance to the Psalms. Furthermore, many passages from the Psalter still have devotional impact on the lives of worshipers in our own day. All of these facts point toward the conclusion that the righteous man described in the Psalter was a primitive model of the salt of the New Testament.

Indisputably, Jesus Christ revealed new dimensions to the concept of saltness. He was, is, and ever shall be the final authority on how to be salt that does not lose its savor. Nevertheless, the representative "righteous man of the Psalter" demonstrated the preservative and zestful qualities of salt according to the best light of his own day.

GOLDEN GATE SEMINARY LIBRARY